I0480910

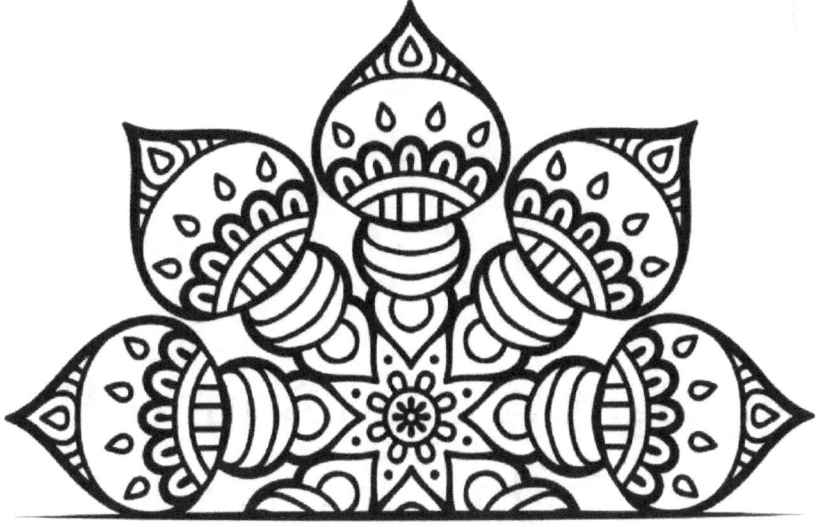

This Book Belongs To:

_____

_____

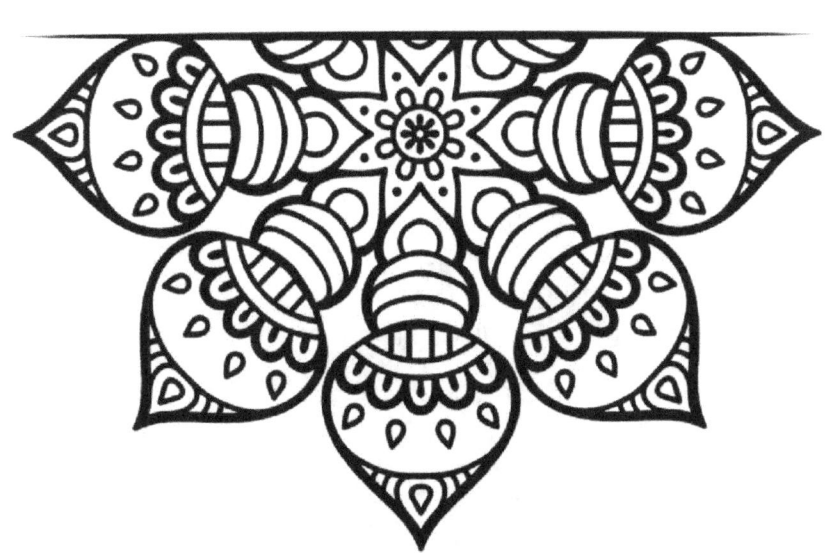

Copyright © 2020 Annett Hill
All Rights Reserved.

No part of this publication may be copied or reproduced in any format, by any means, including electronic methods, without the prior written permission of the publisher of this book.

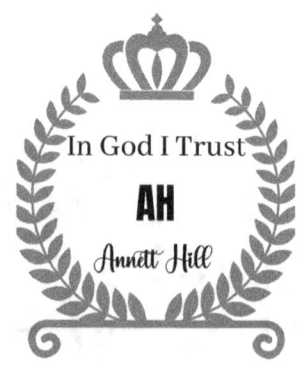

INTENTIONALLY LEFT BLANK

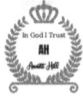 **ANNETT HILL**

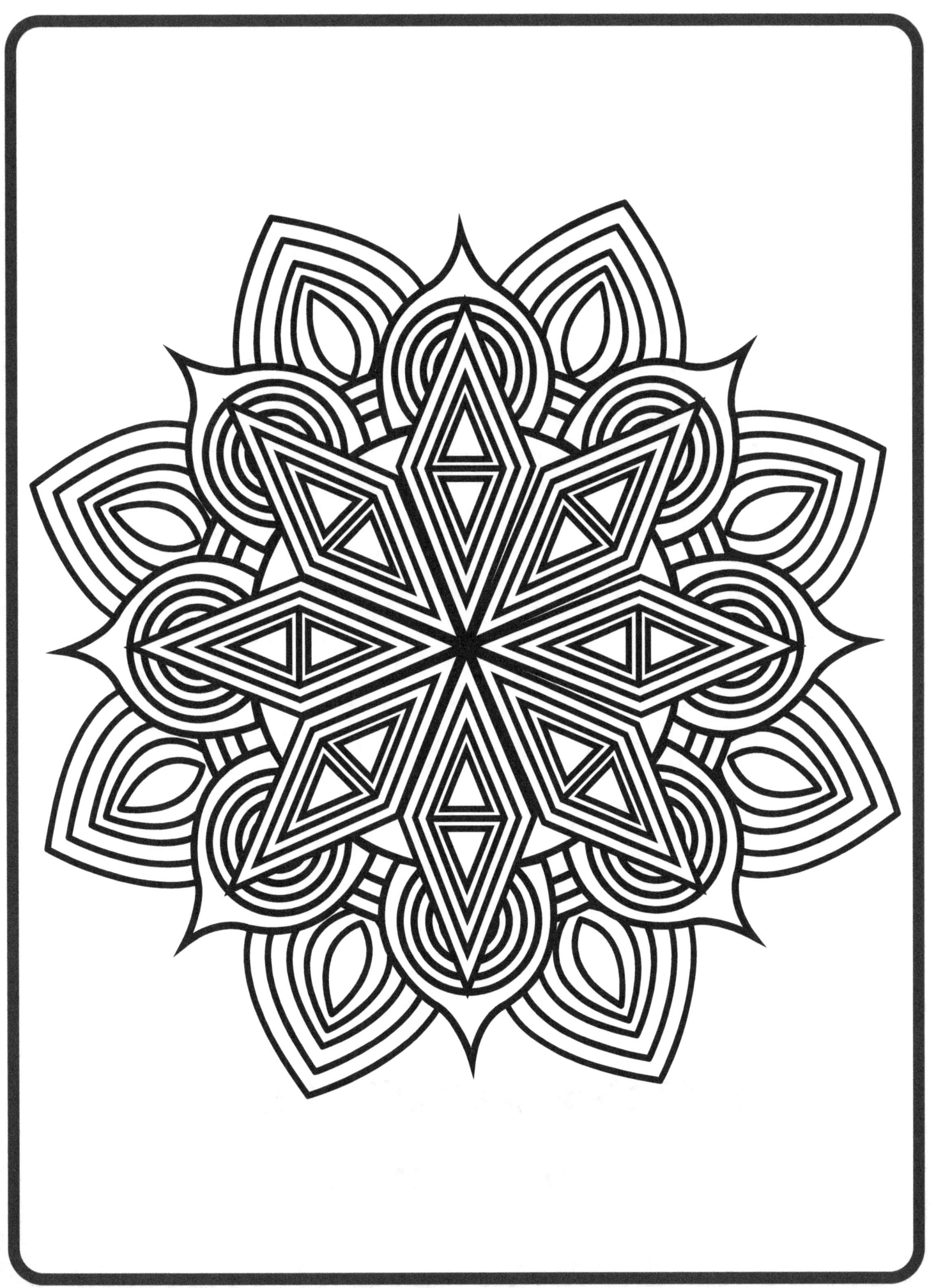

INTENTIONALLY LEFT BLANK

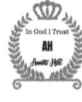 **ANNETT HILL**

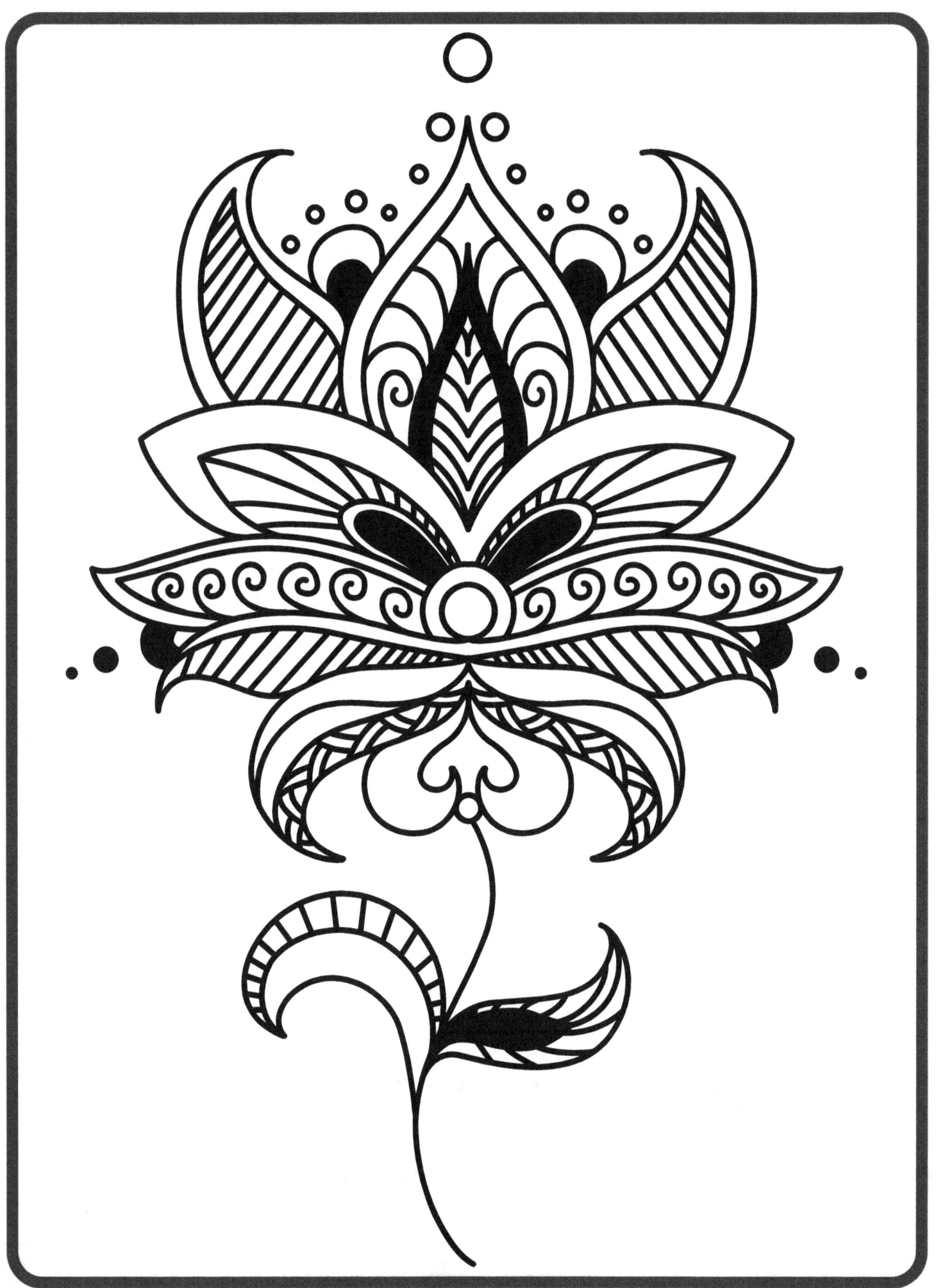

INTENTIONALLY LEFT BLANK

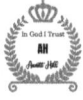 ANNETT HILL

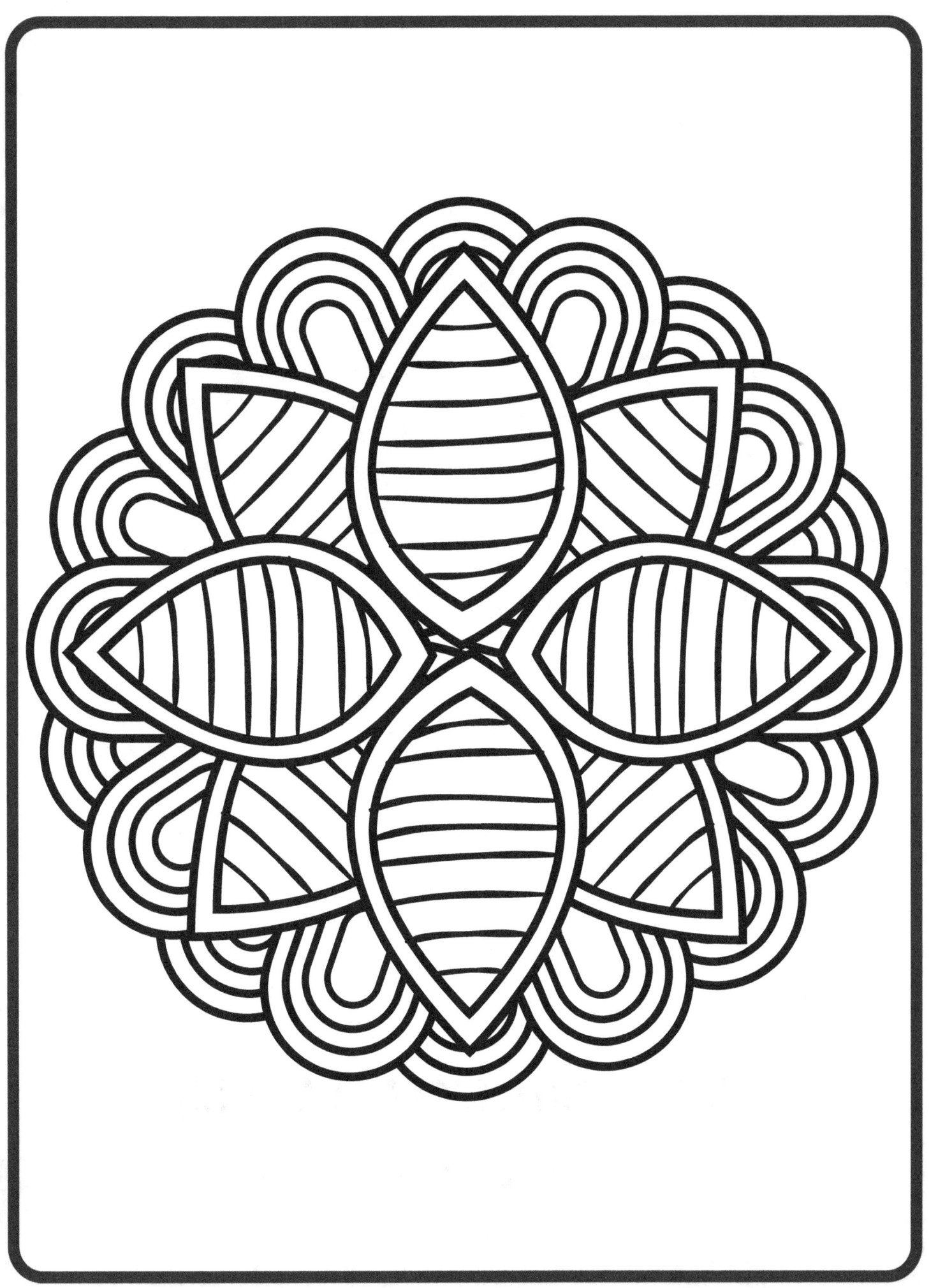

INTENTIONALLY LEFT BLANK

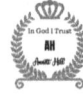 **ANNETT HILL**

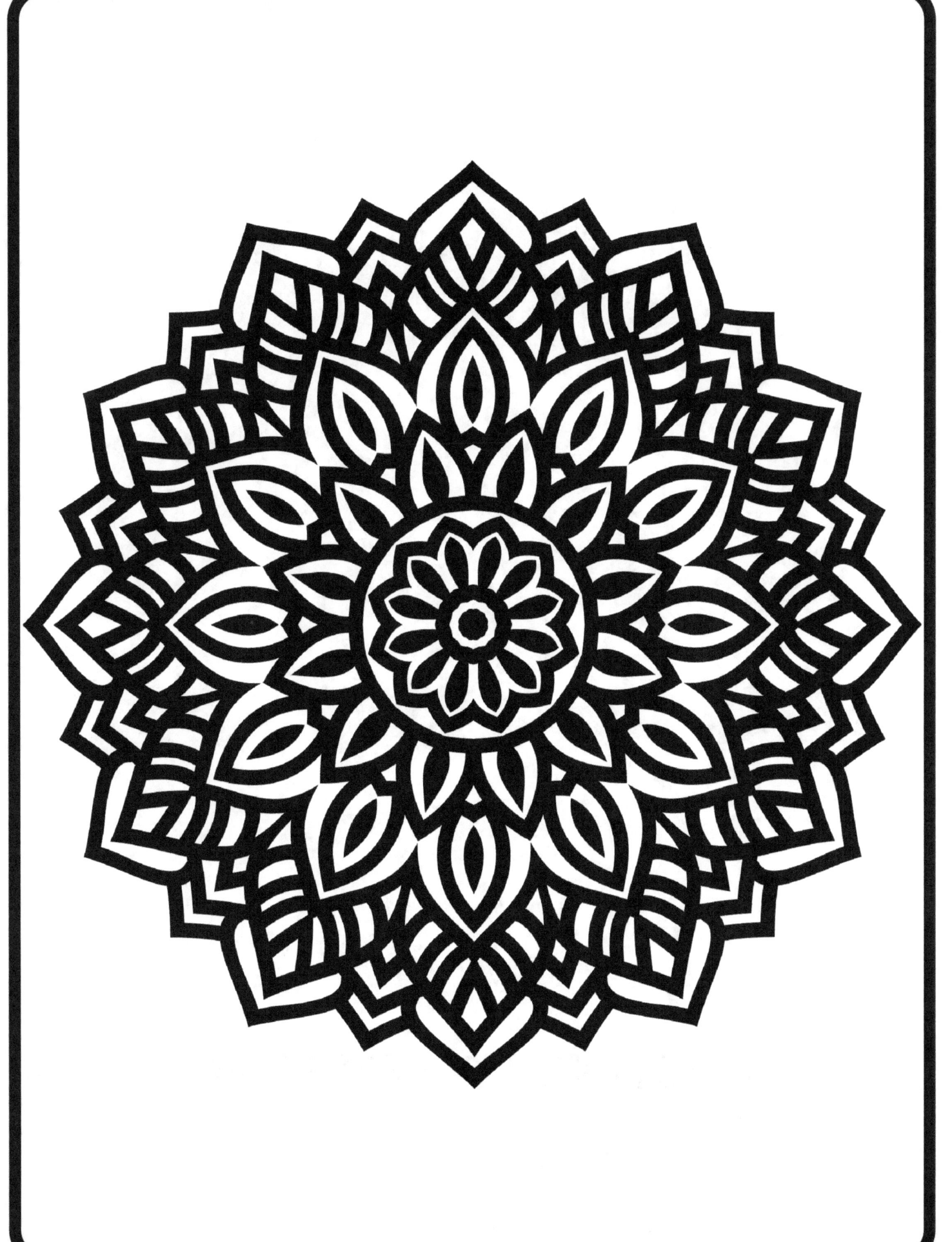

INTENTIONALLY LEFT BLANK

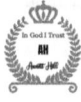 **ANNETT HILL**

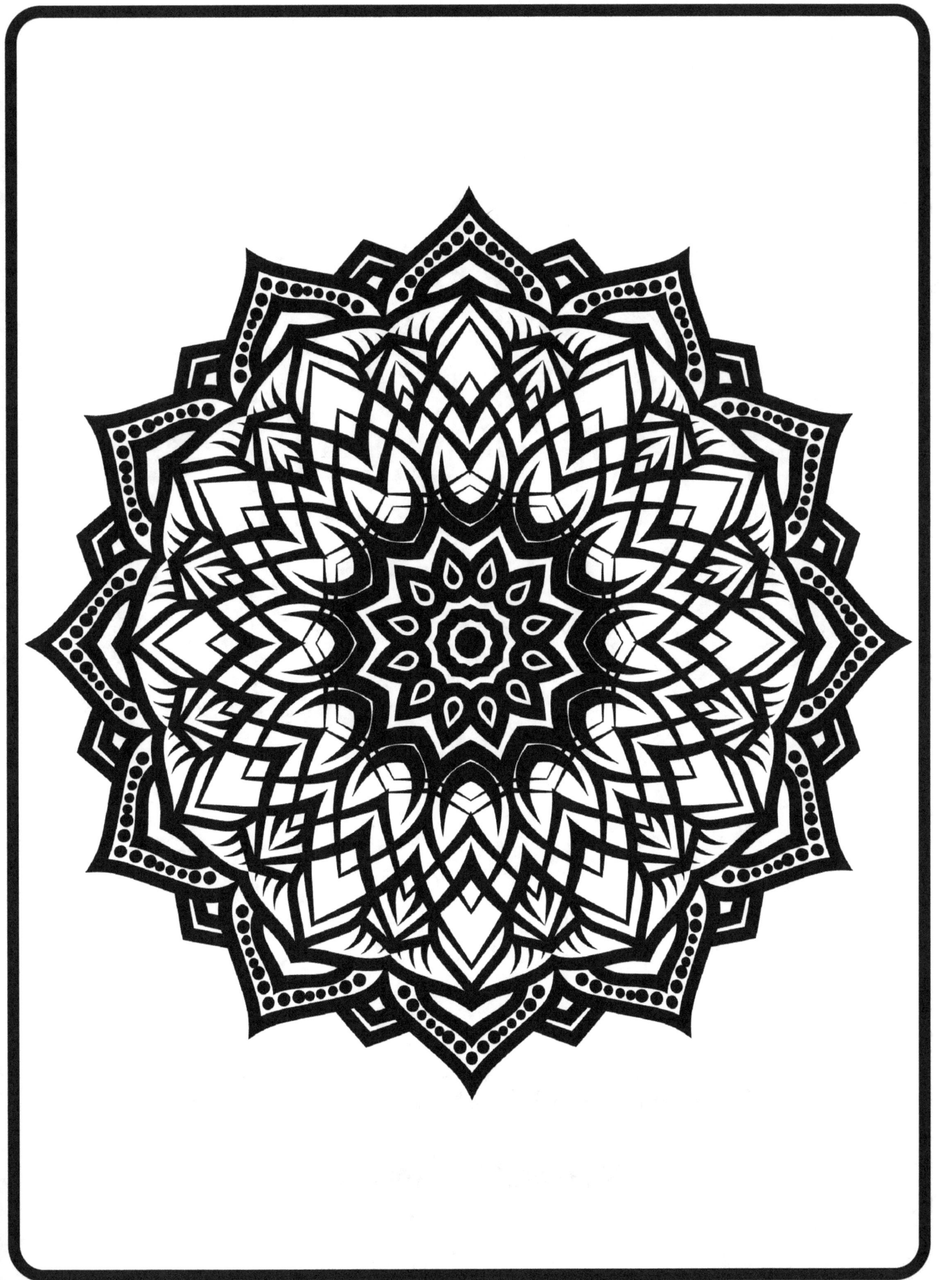

INTENTIONALLY LEFT BLANK

 **ANNETT HILL**

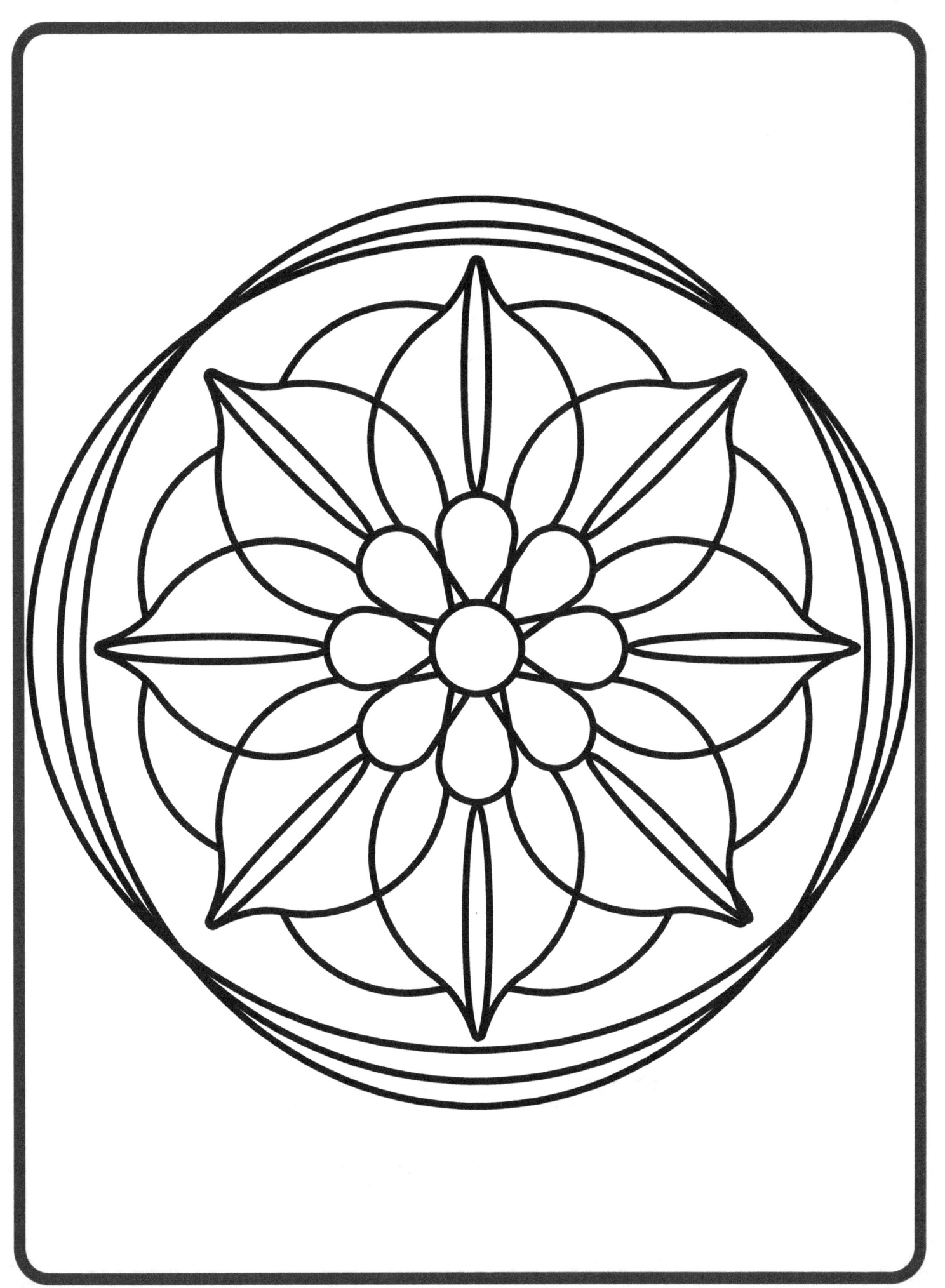

INTENTIONALLY LEFT BLANK

 ANNETT HILL

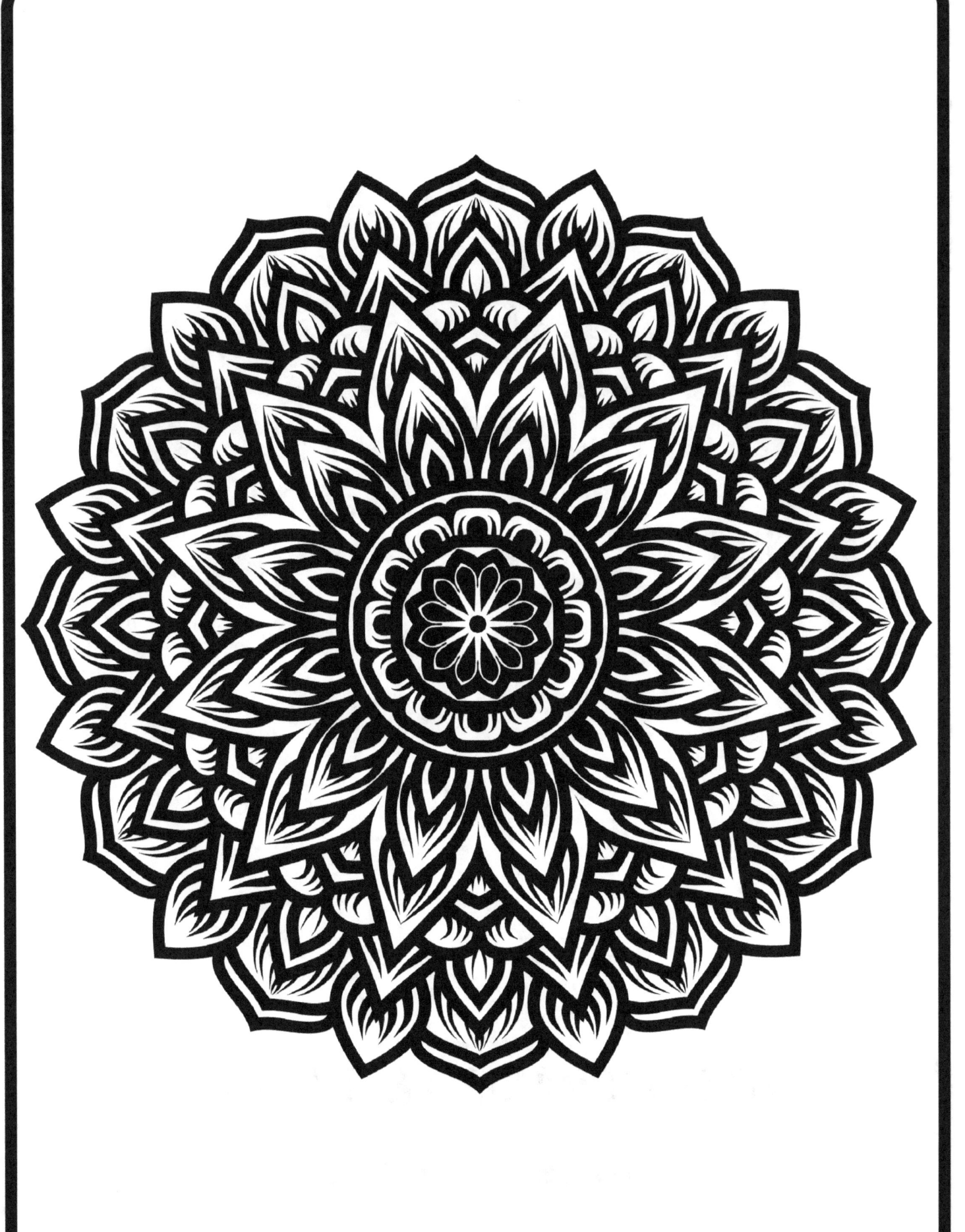

INTENTIONALLY LEFT BLANK

 ANNETT HILL

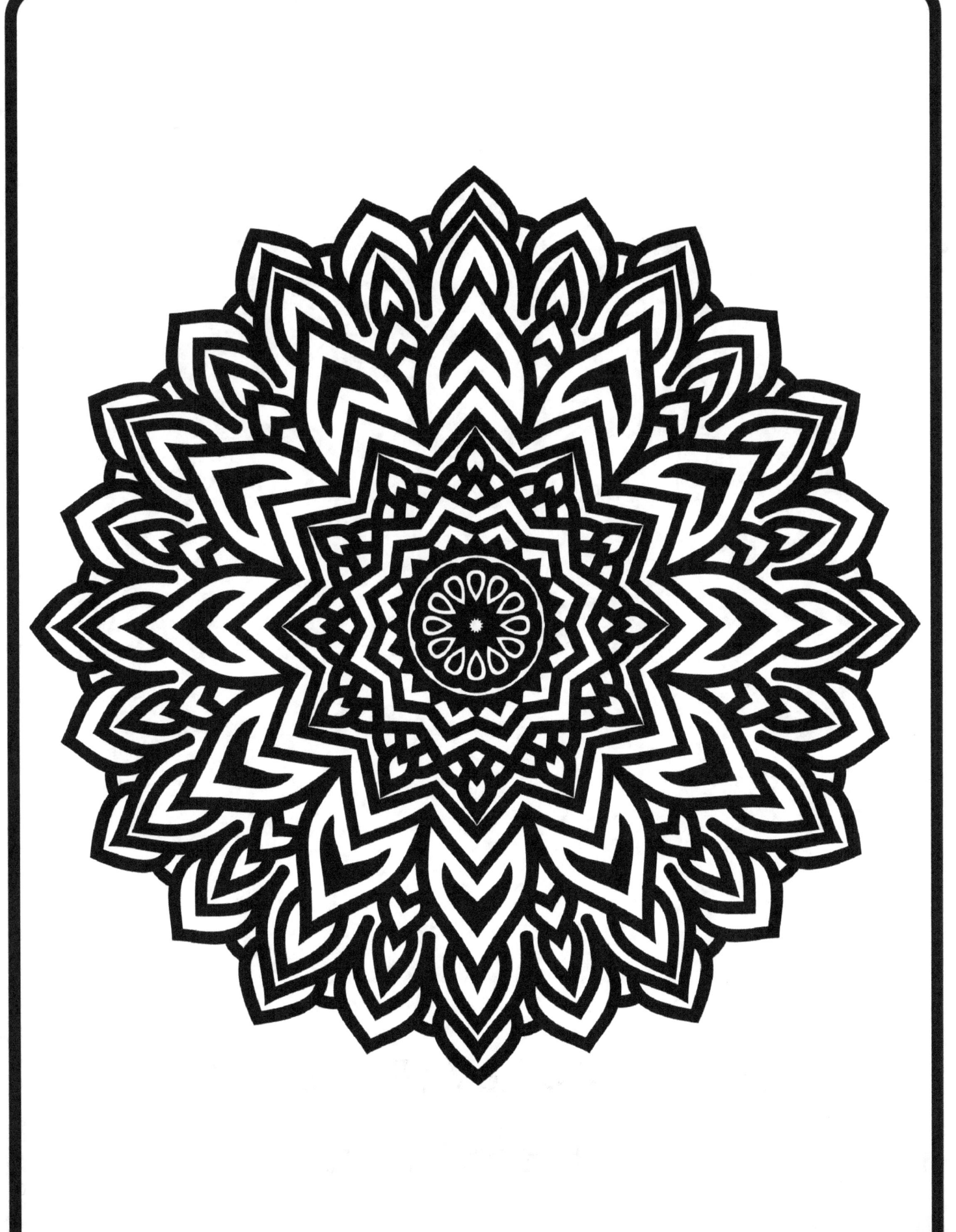

INTENTIONALLY LEFT BLANK

 ANNETT HILL

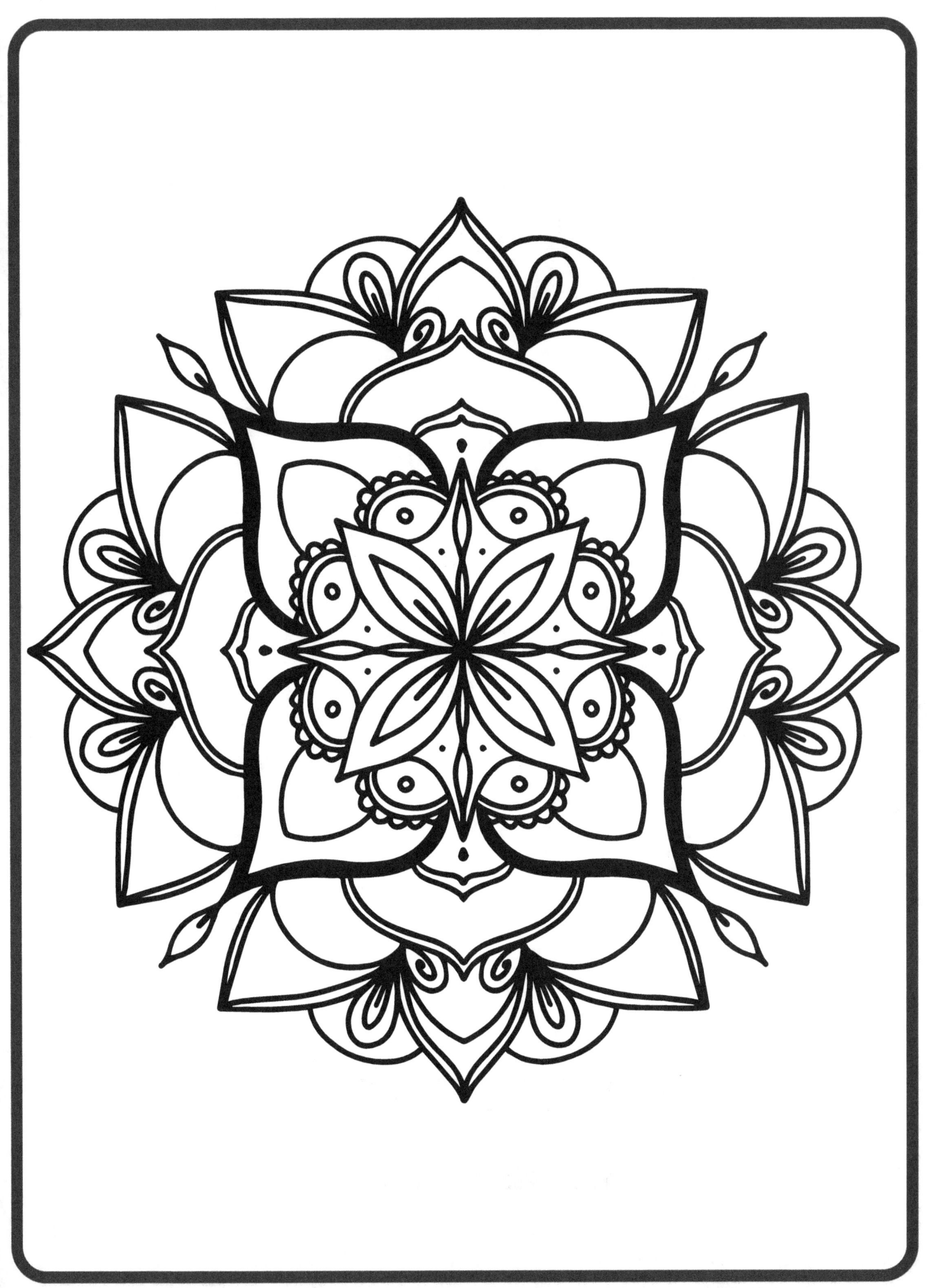

INTENTIONALLY LEFT BLANK

 ANNETT HILL

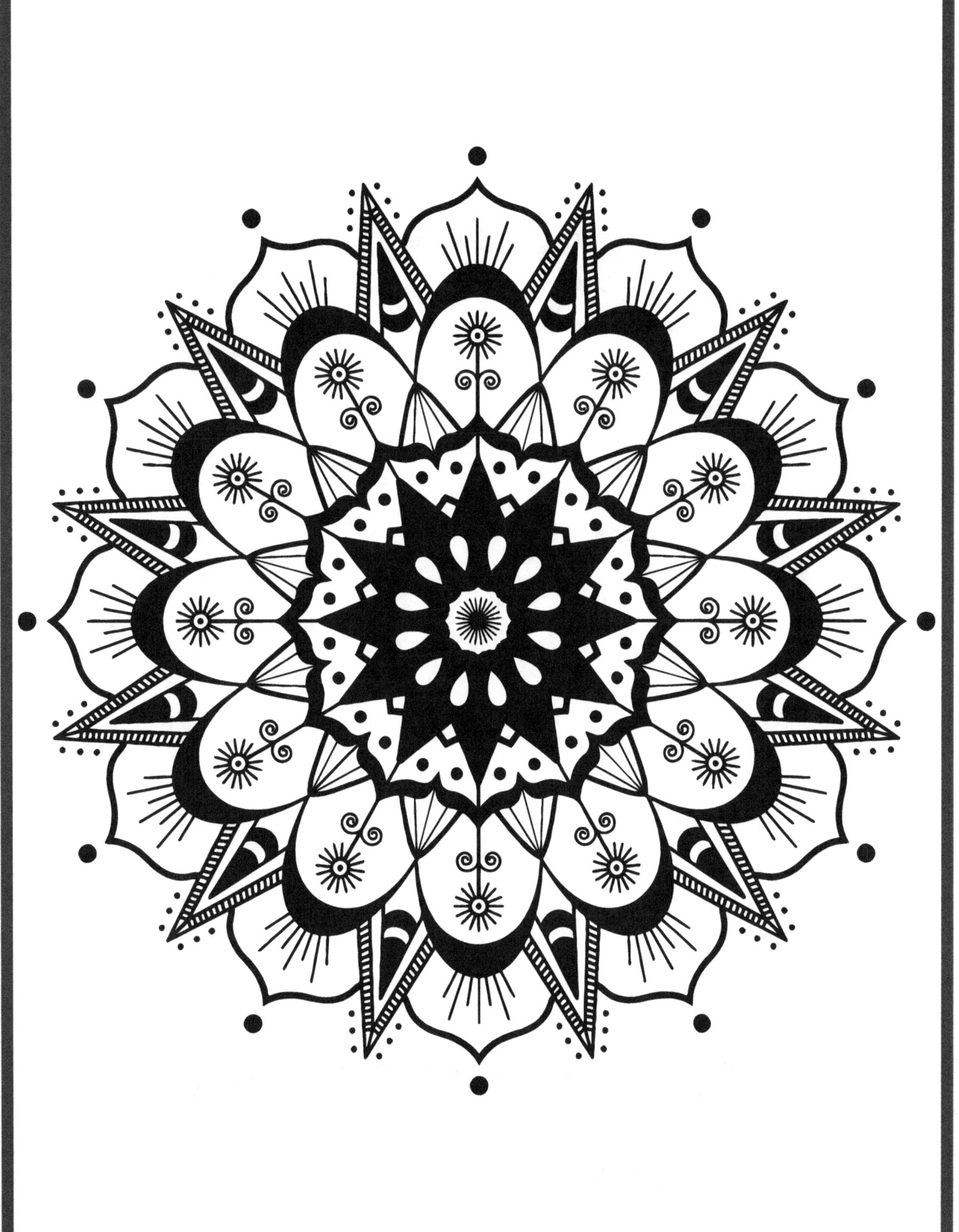

INTENTIONALLY LEFT BLANK

 ANNETT HILL

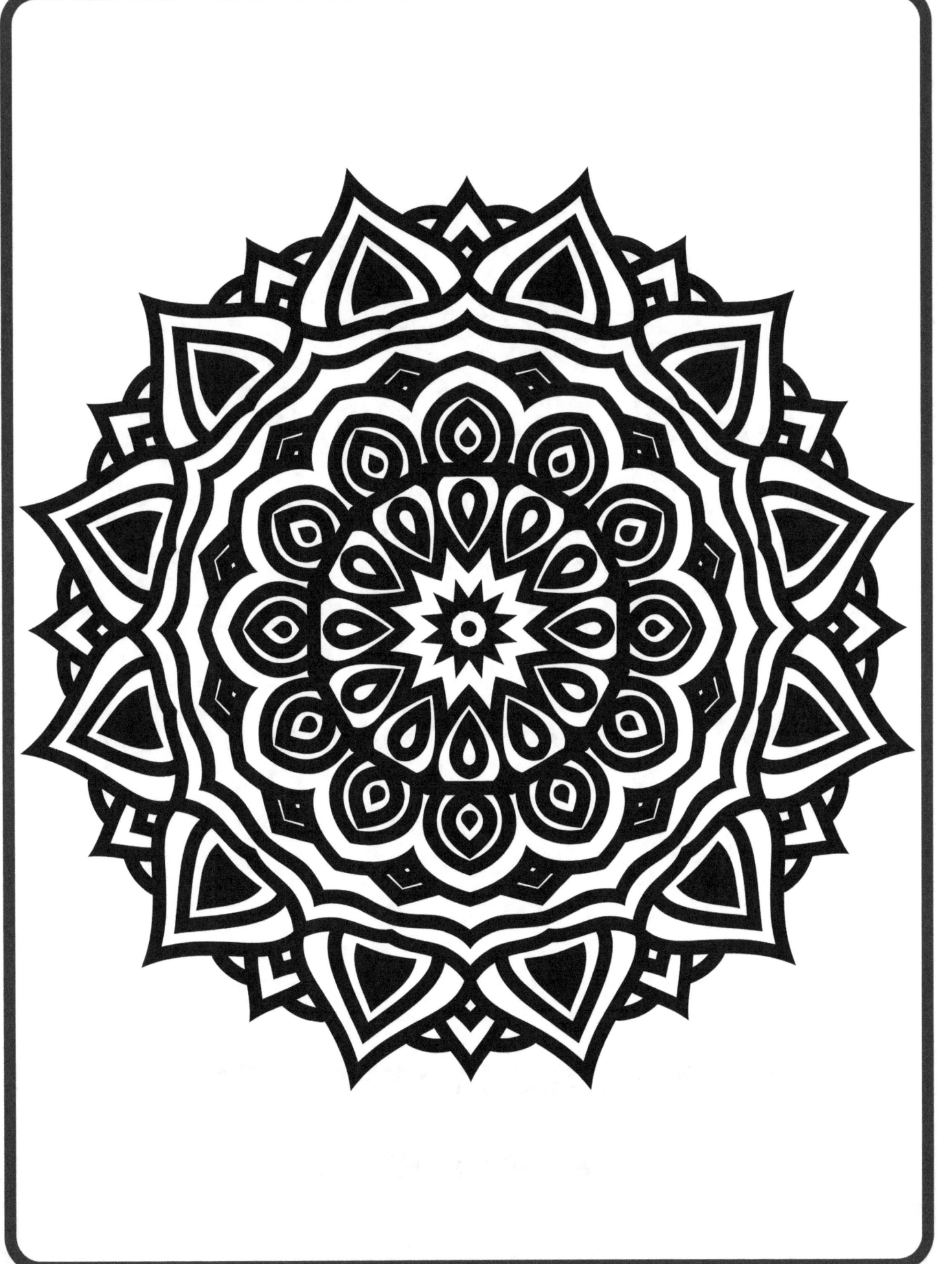

INTENTIONALLY LEFT BLANK

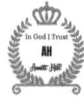 **ANNETT HILL**

INTENTIONALLY LEFT BLANK

 ANNETT HILL

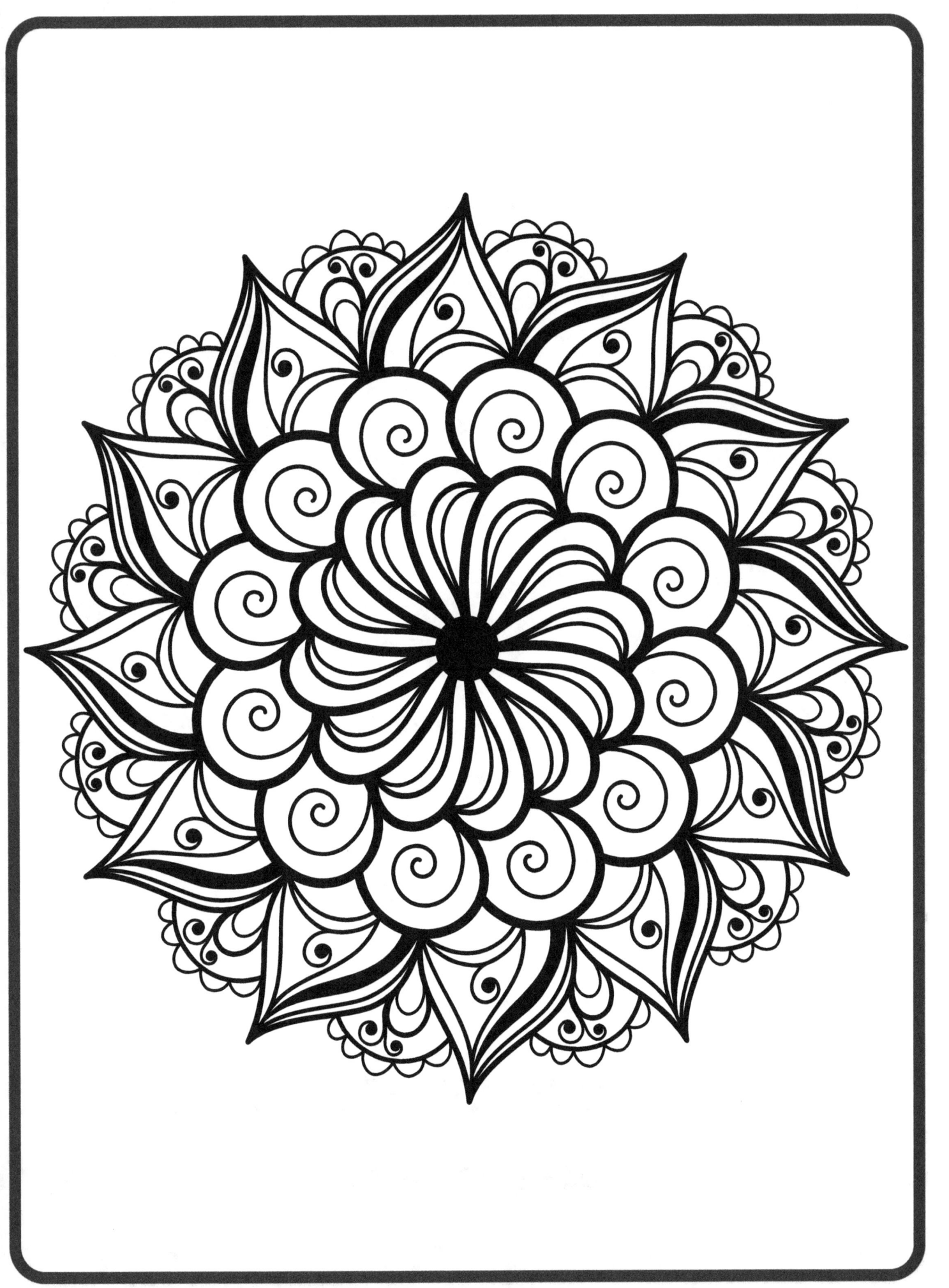

INTENTIONALLY LEFT BLANK

 ANNETT HILL

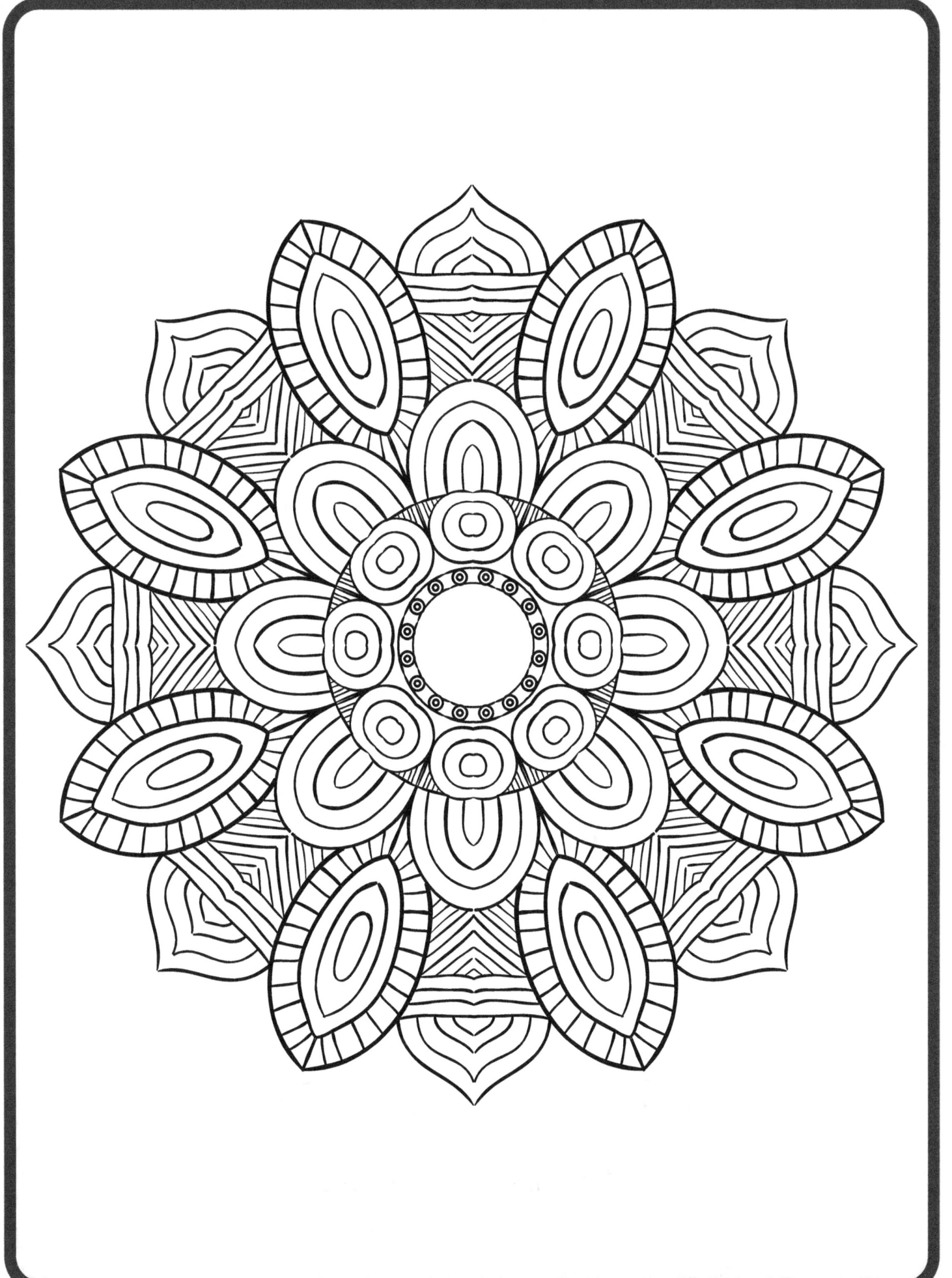

INTENTIONALLY LEFT BLANK

 ANNETT HILL

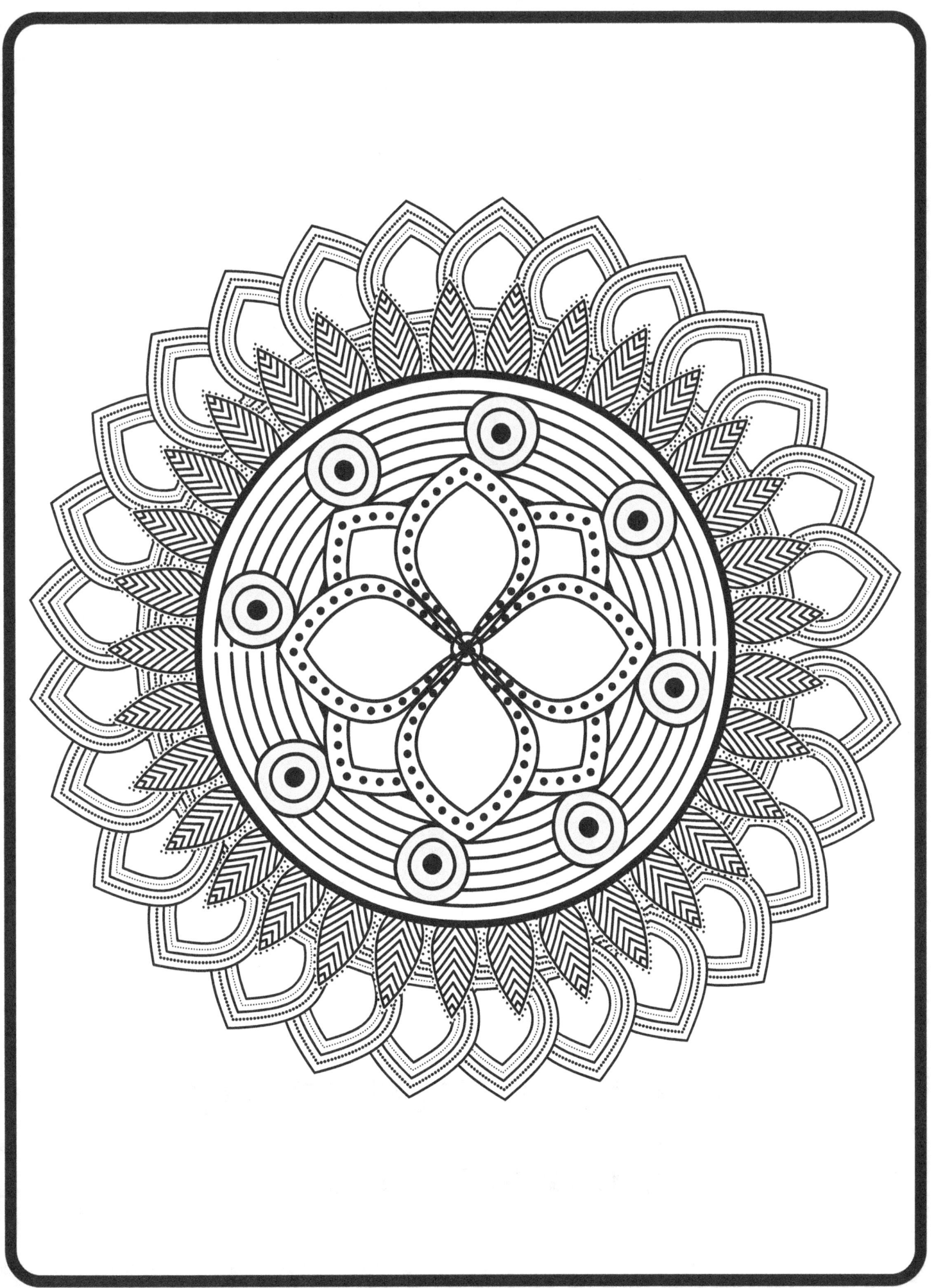

INTENTIONALLY LEFT BLANK

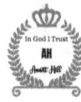 **ANNETT HILL**

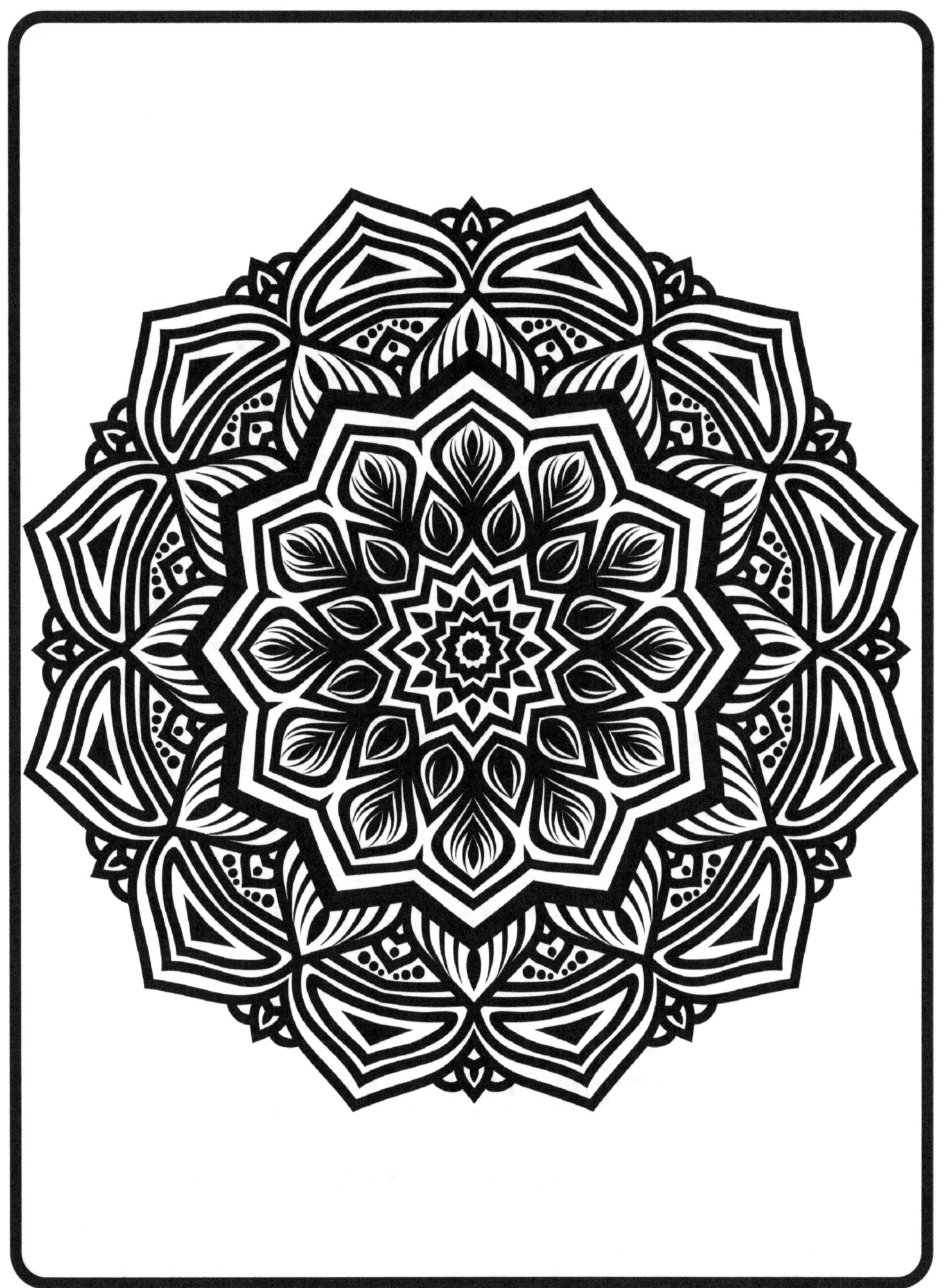

INTENTIONALLY LEFT BLANK

 ANNETT HILL

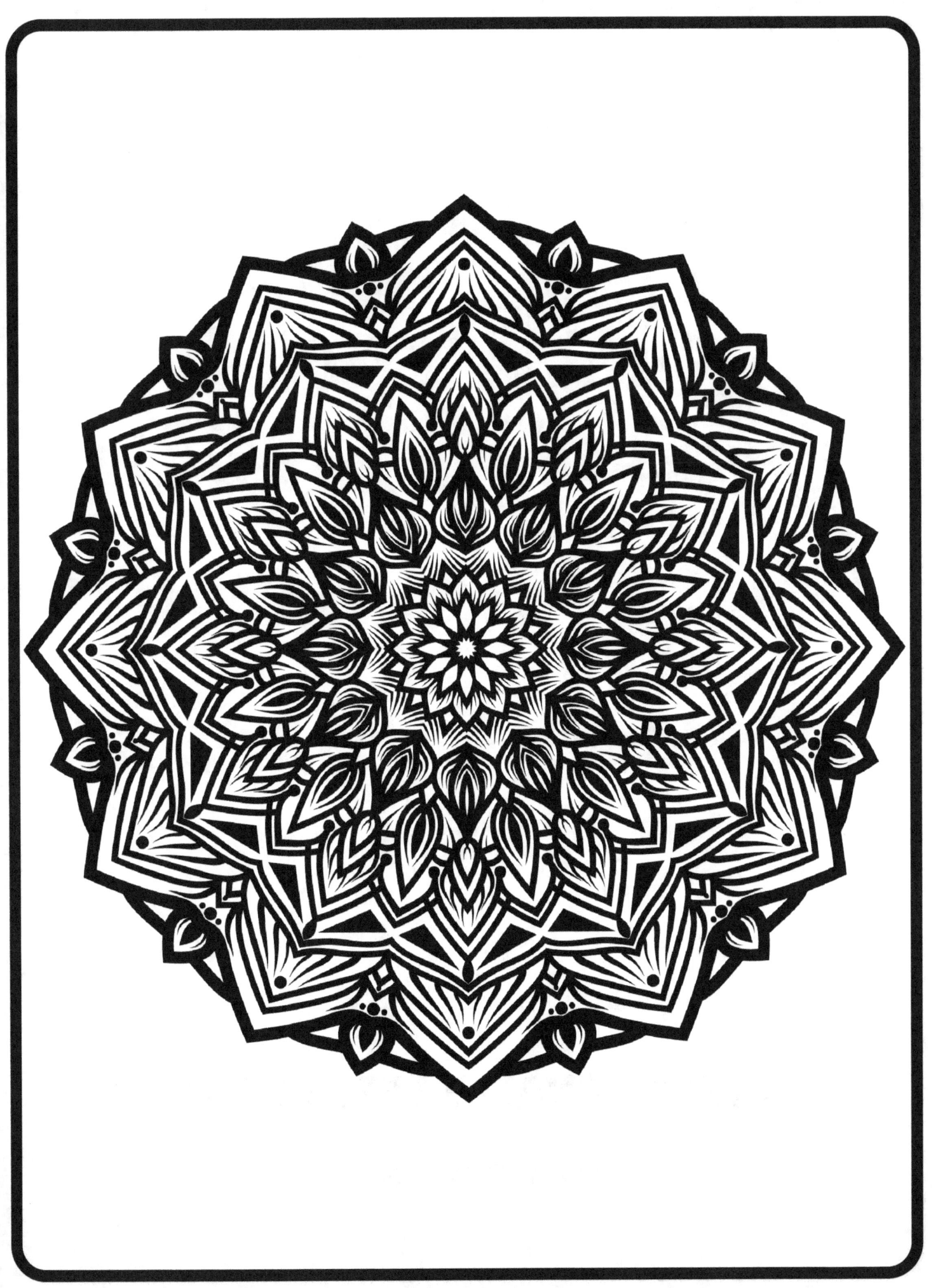

INTENTIONALLY LEFT BLANK

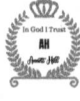 ANNETT HILL

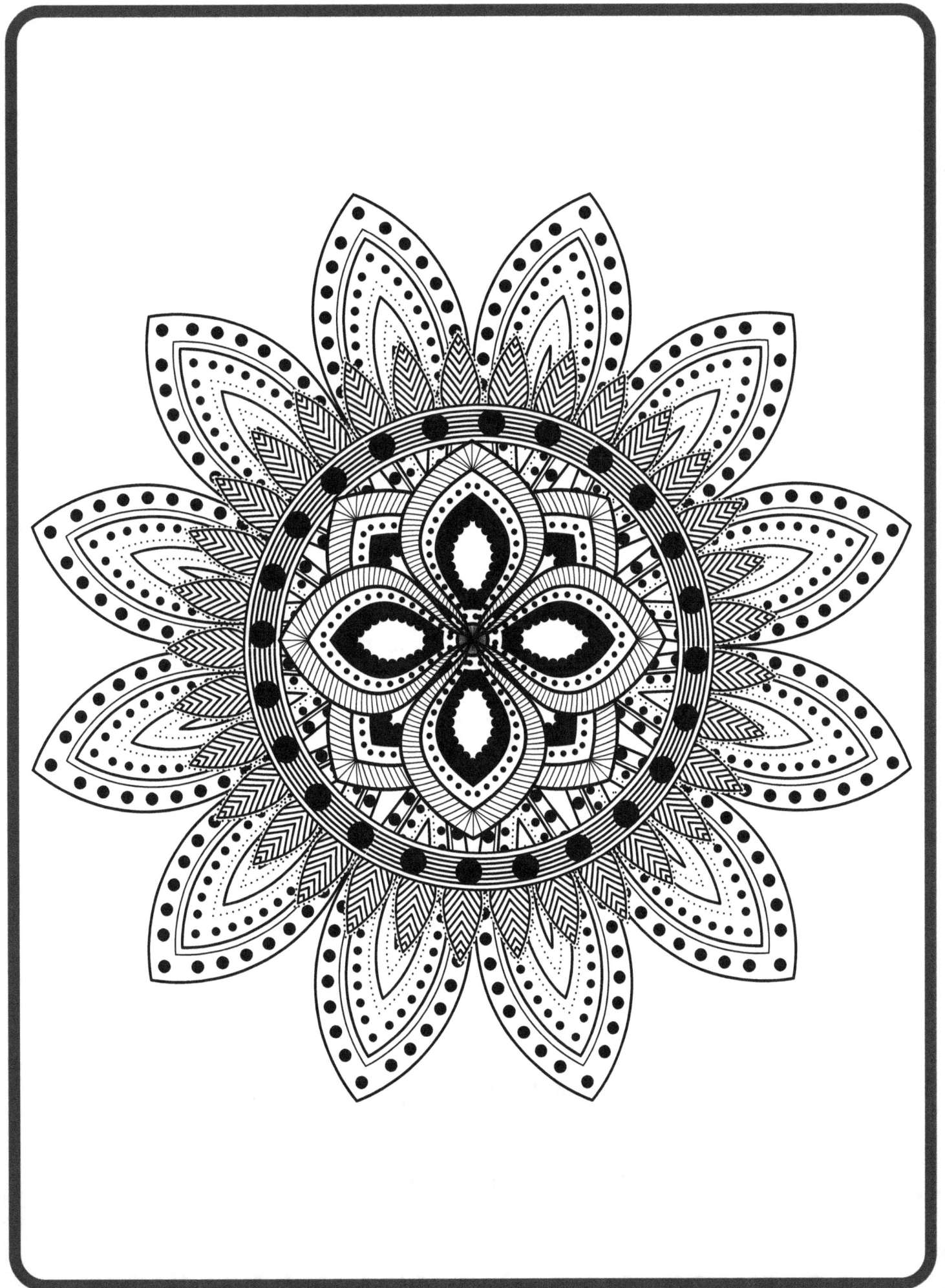

INTENTIONALLY LEFT BLANK

 ANNETT HILL

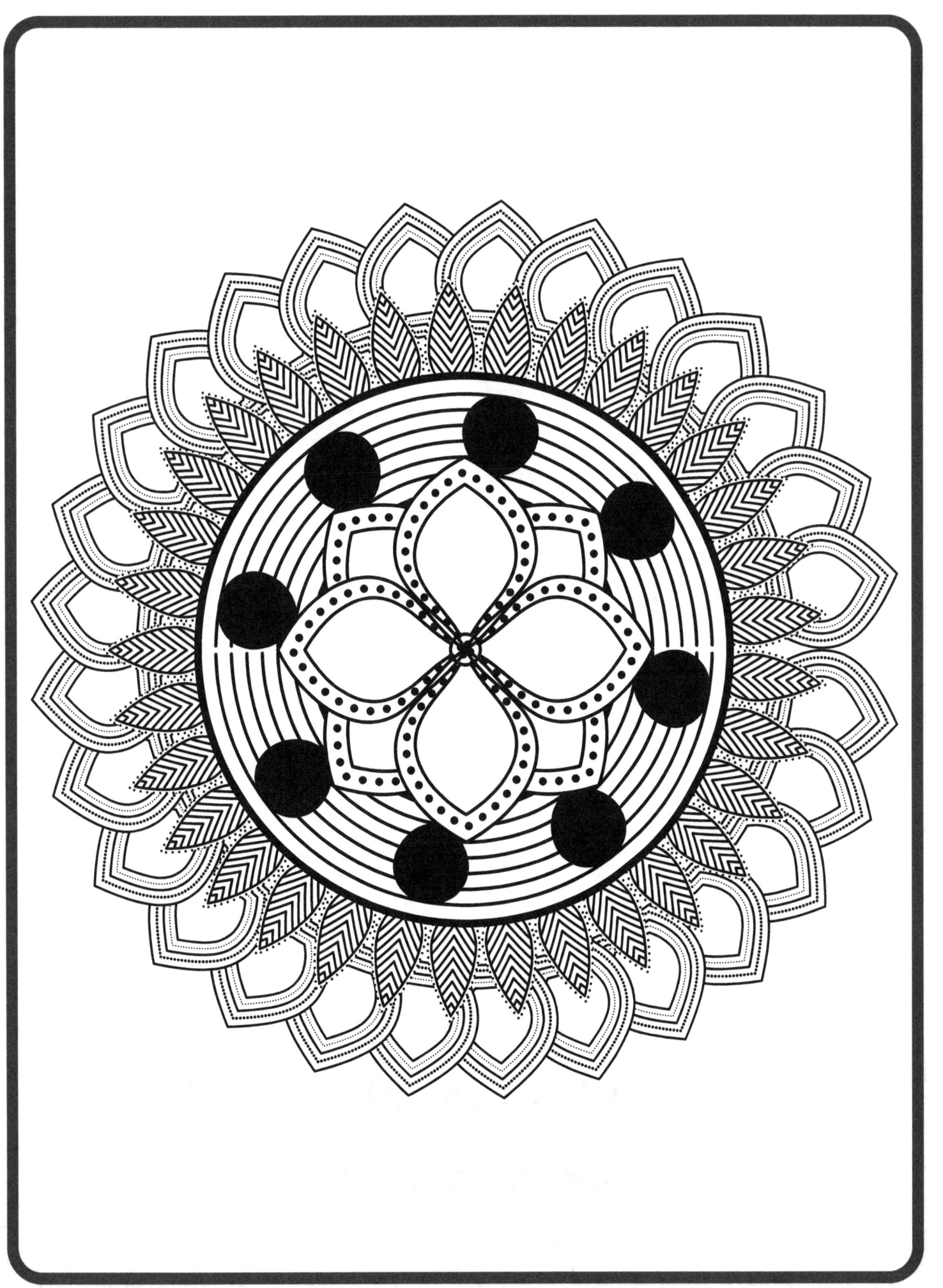

INTENTIONALLY LEFT BLANK

 ANNETT HILL

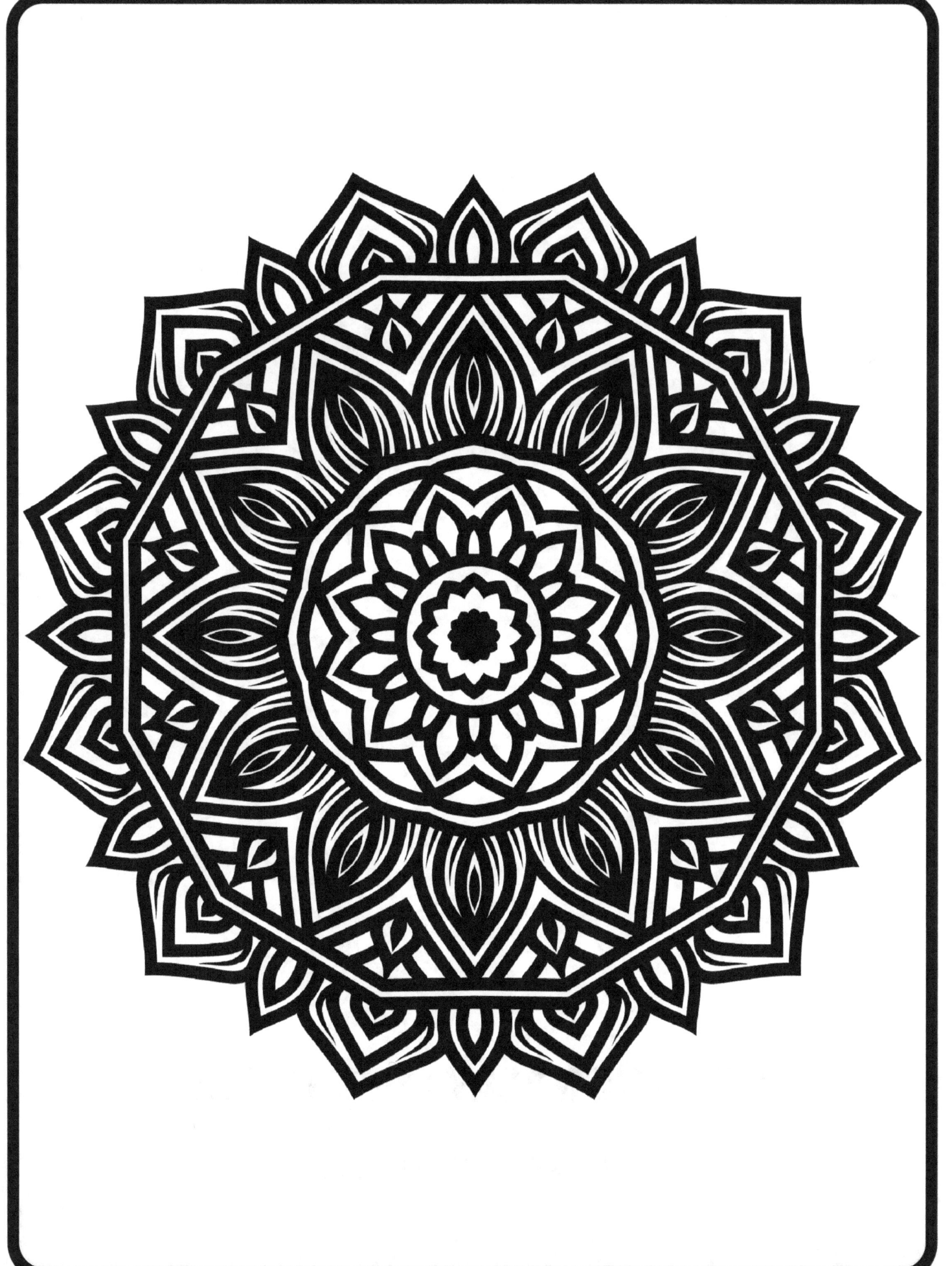

INTENTIONALLY LEFT BLANK

 ANNETT HILL

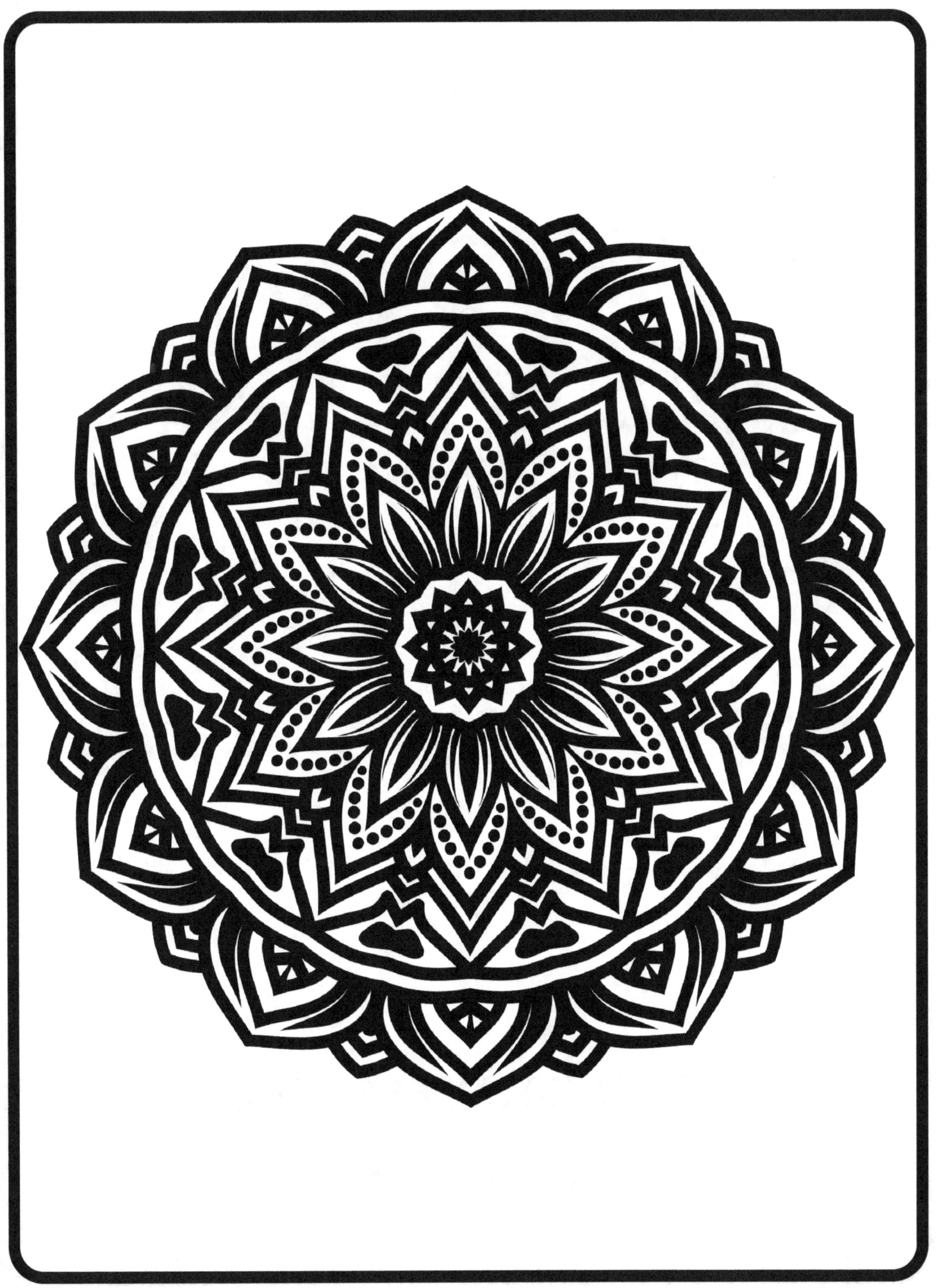

INTENTIONALLY LEFT BLANK

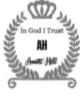 **ANNETT HILL**

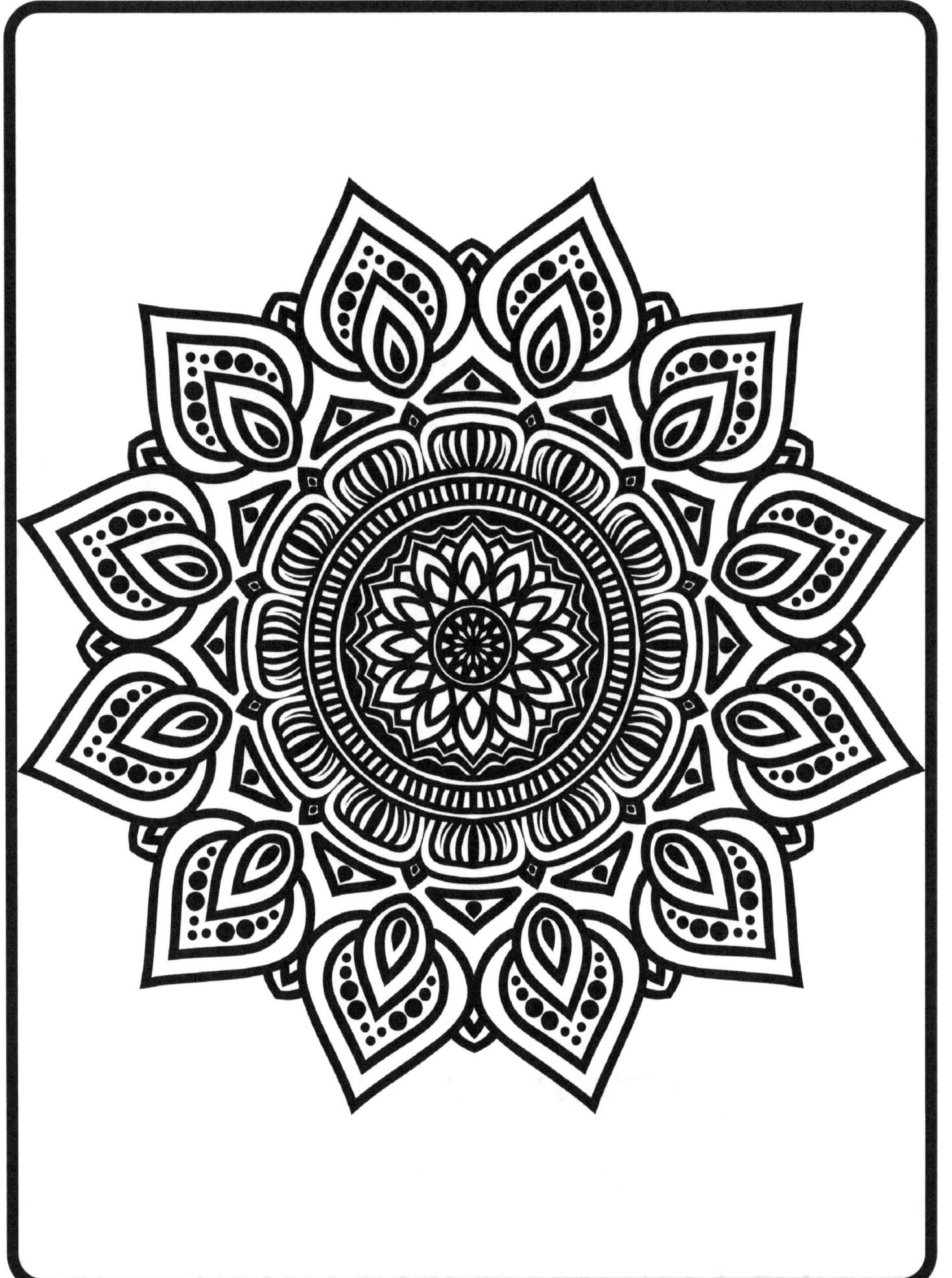

INTENTIONALLY LEFT BLANK

 ANNETT HILL

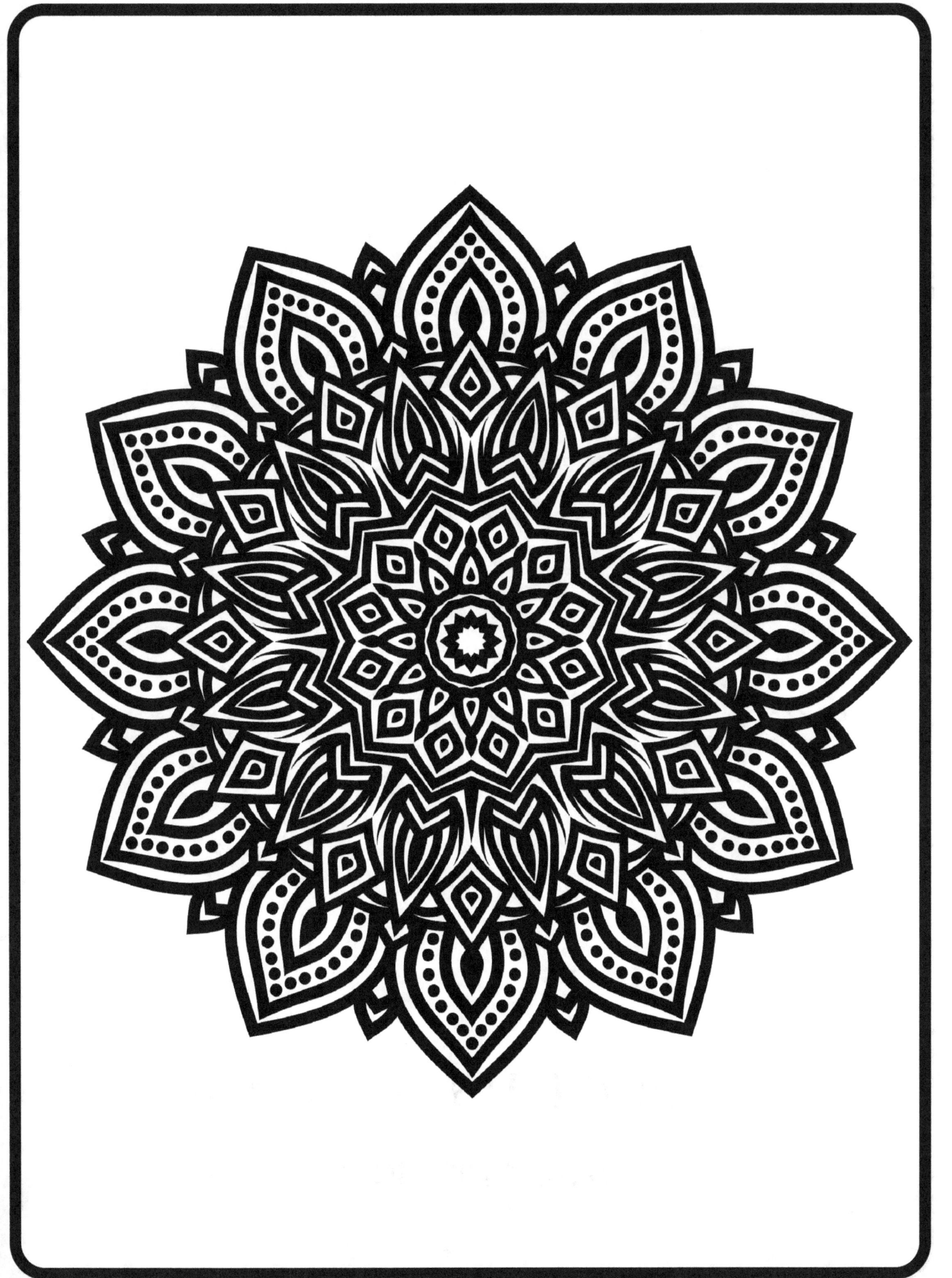

INTENTIONALLY LEFT BLANK

 ANNETT HILL

INTENTIONALLY LEFT BLANK

 ANNETT HILL

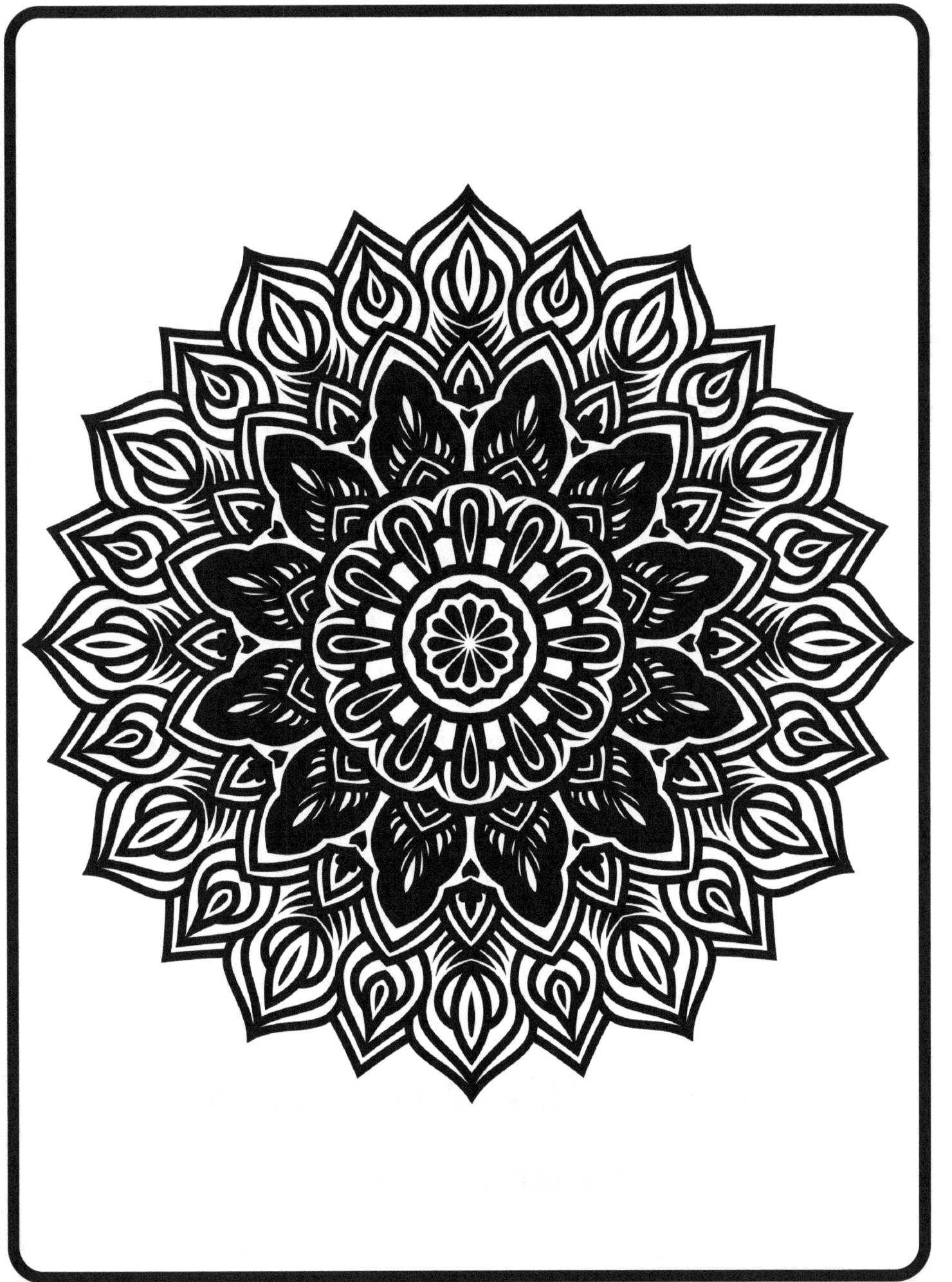

INTENTIONALLY LEFT BLANK

 ANNETT HILL

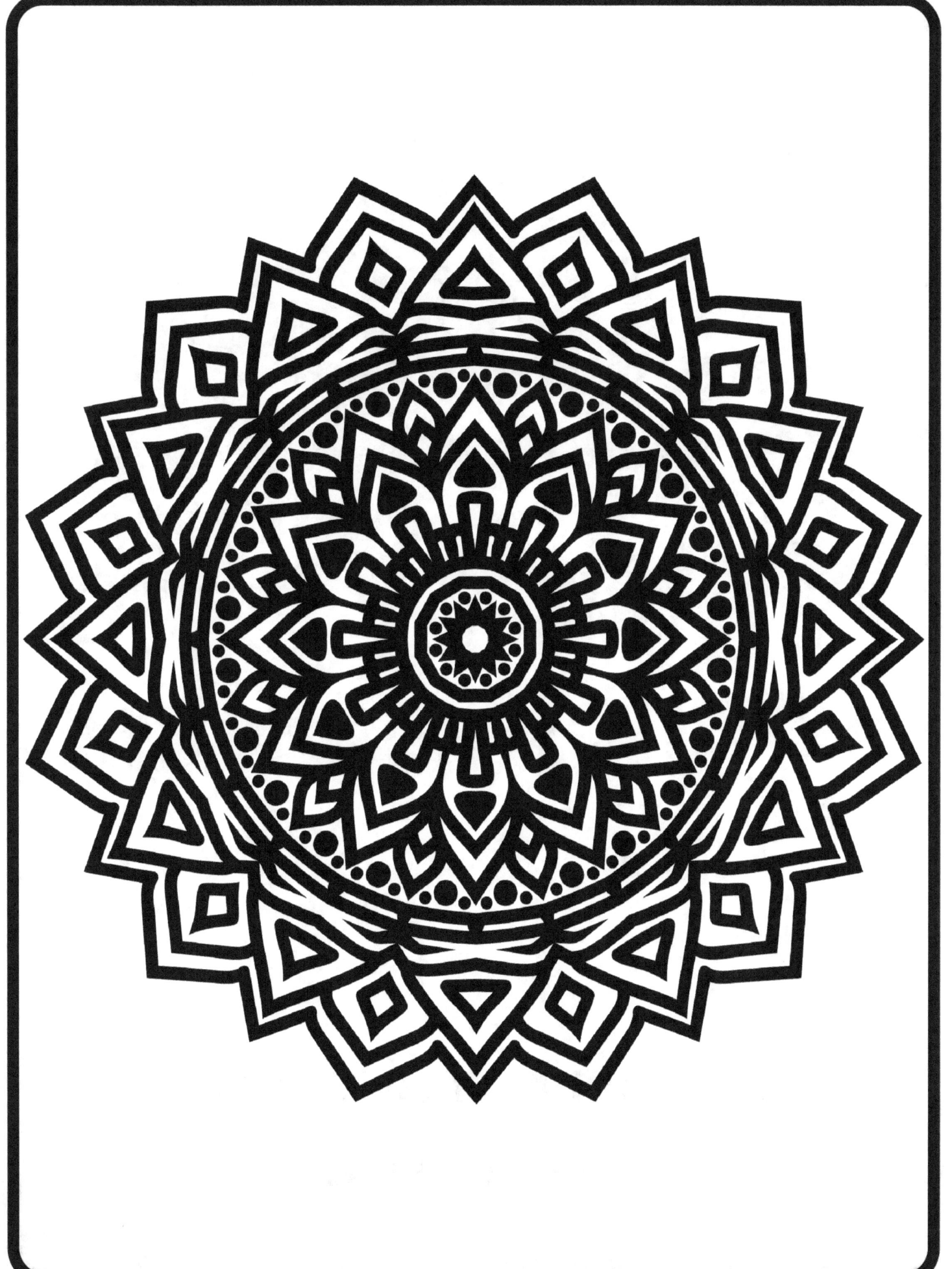

INTENTIONALLY LEFT BLANK

 ANNETT HILL

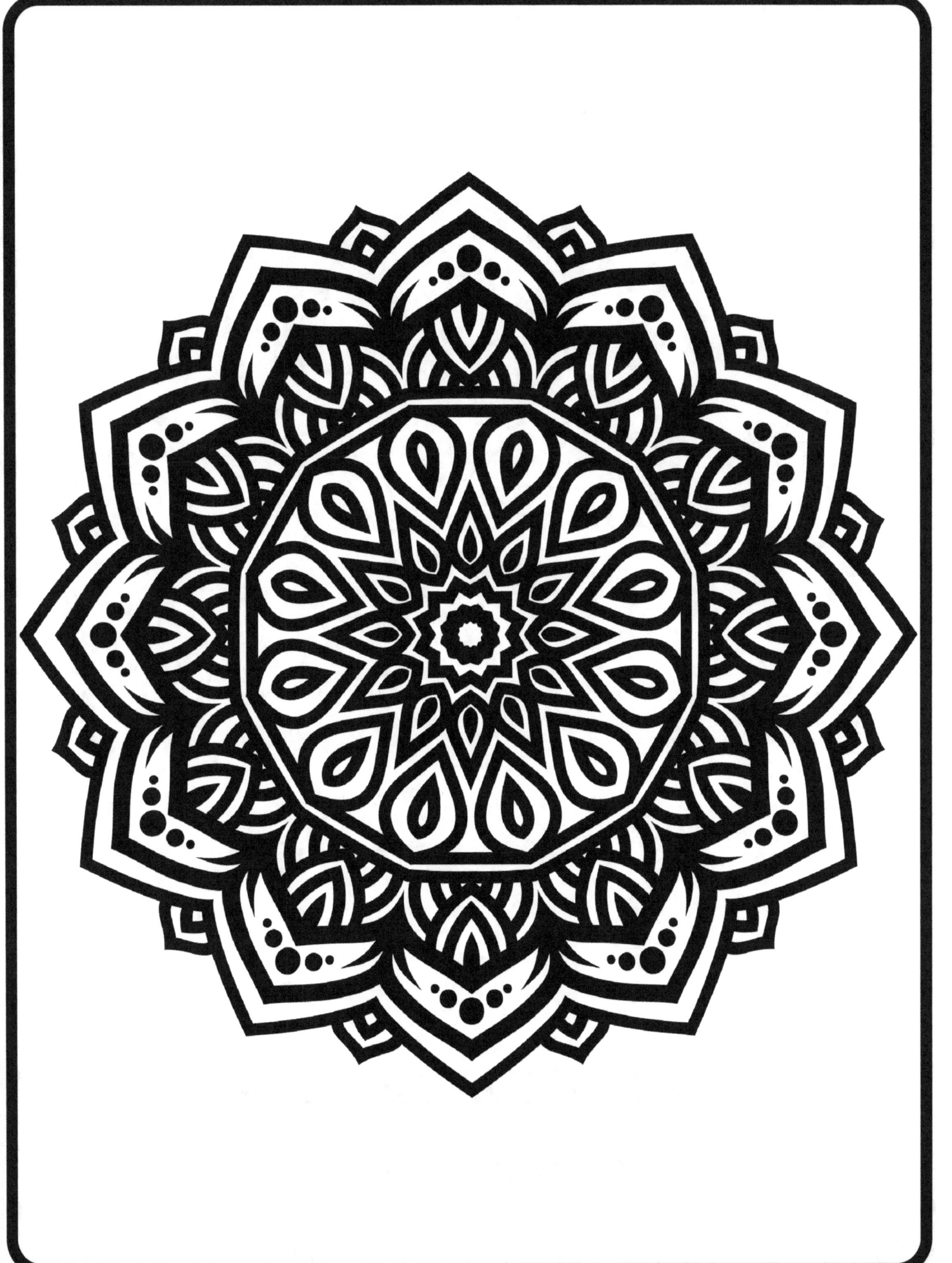

INTENTIONALLY LEFT BLANK

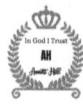 ANNETT HILL

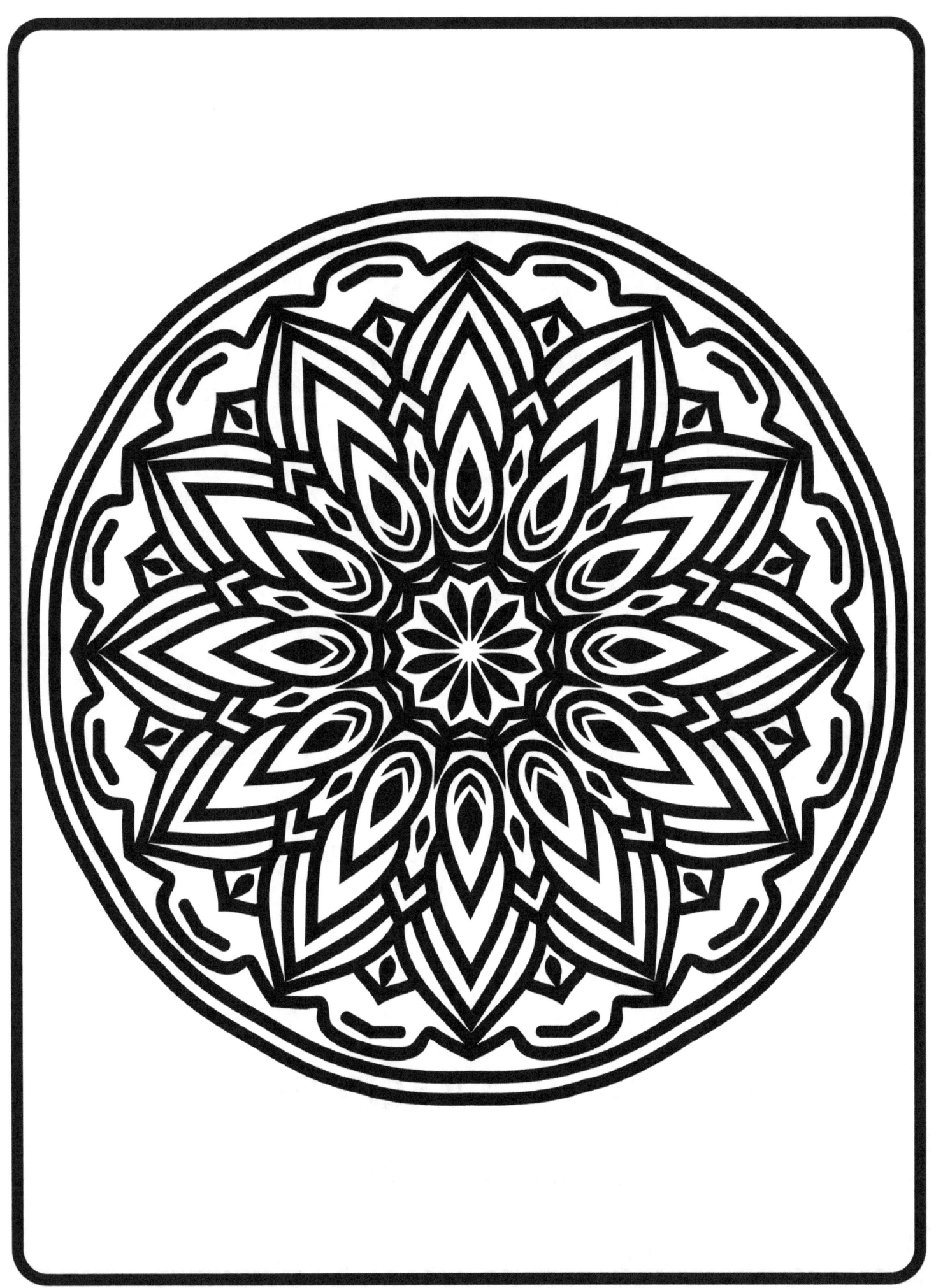

INTENTIONALLY LEFT BLANK

 ANNETT HILL

INTENTIONALLY LEFT BLANK

 ANNETT HILL

INTENTIONALLY LEFT BLANK

 ANNETT HILL

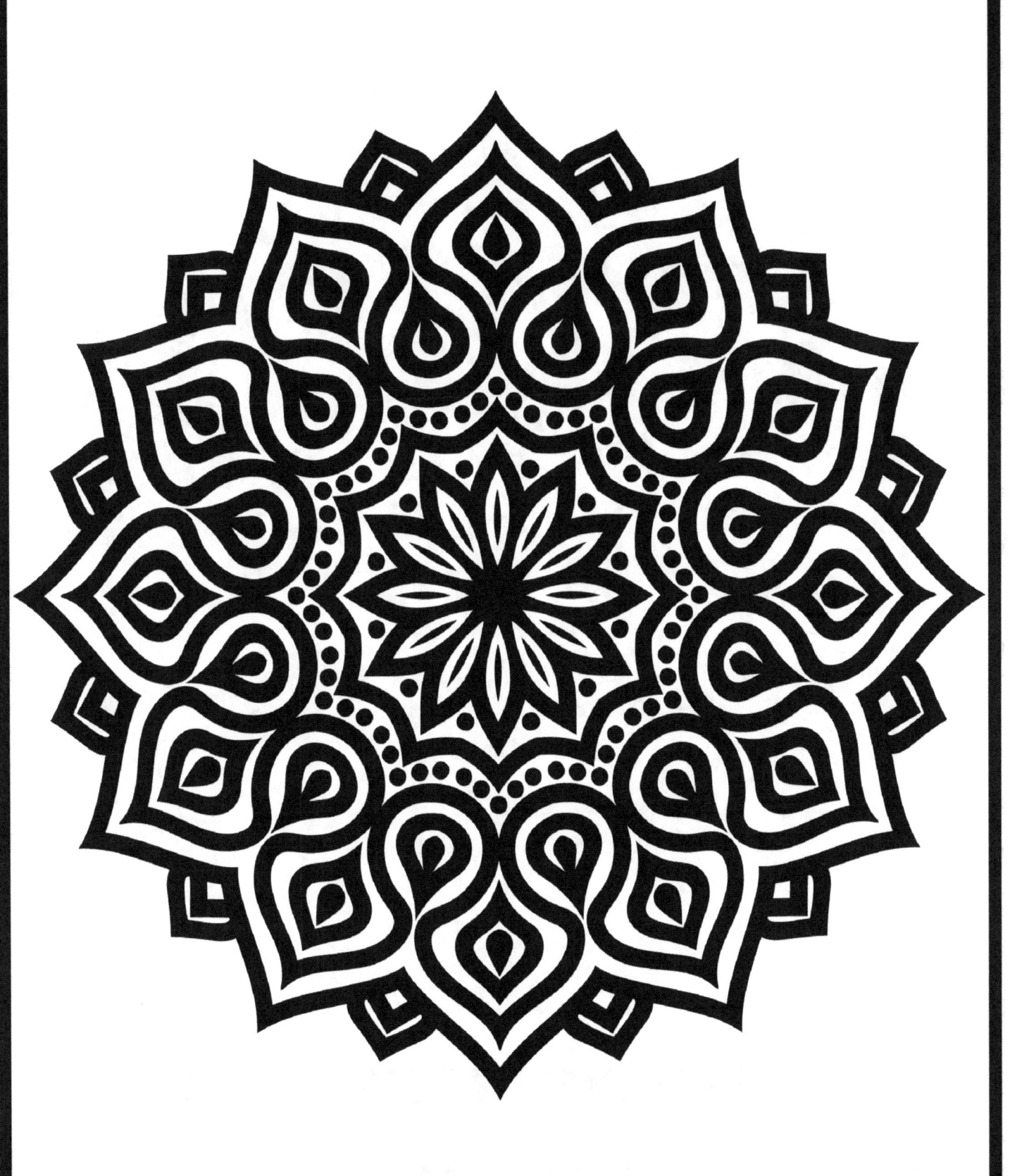

INTENTIONALLY LEFT BLANK

 ANNETT HILL

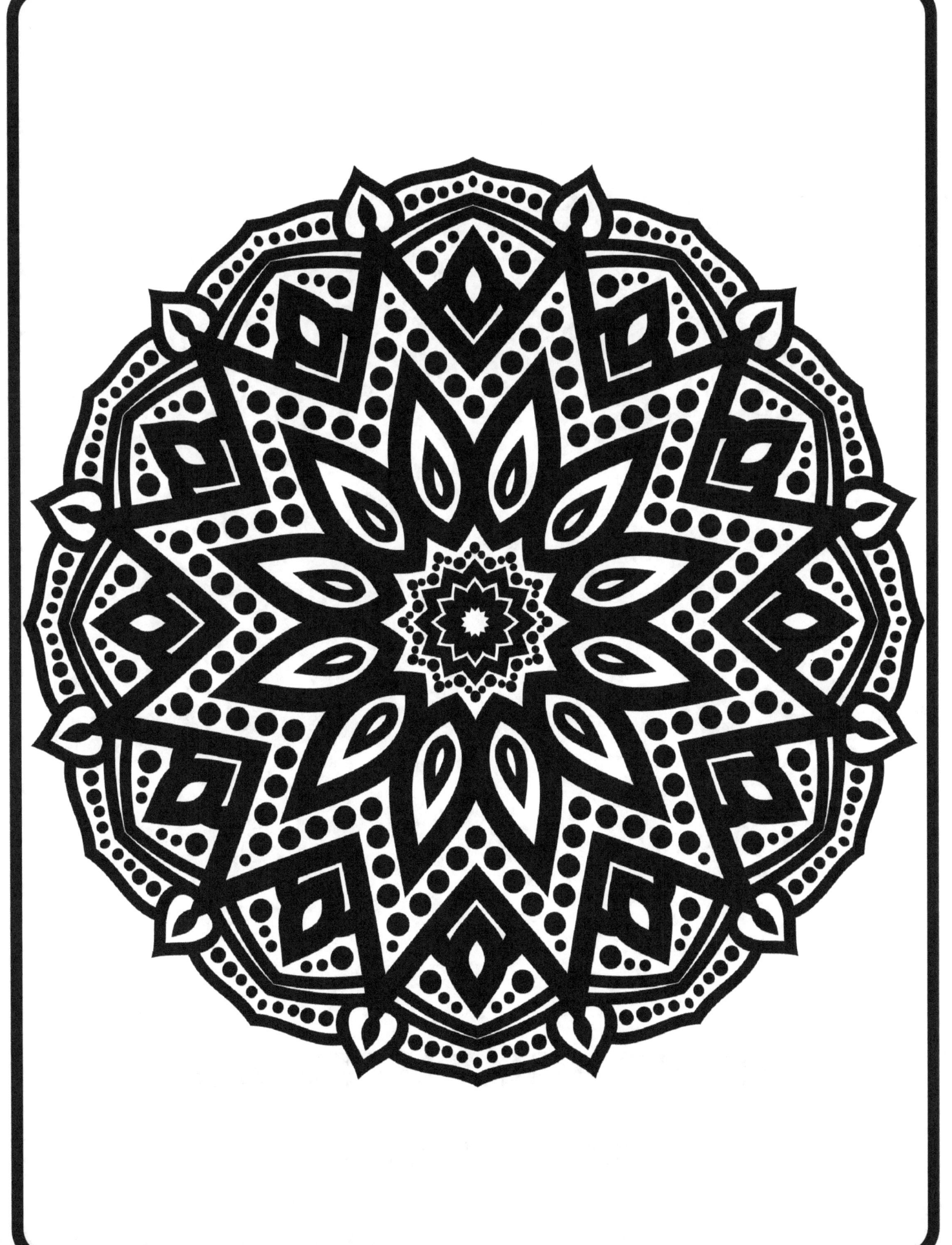

INTENTIONALLY LEFT BLANK

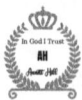 **ANNETT HILL**

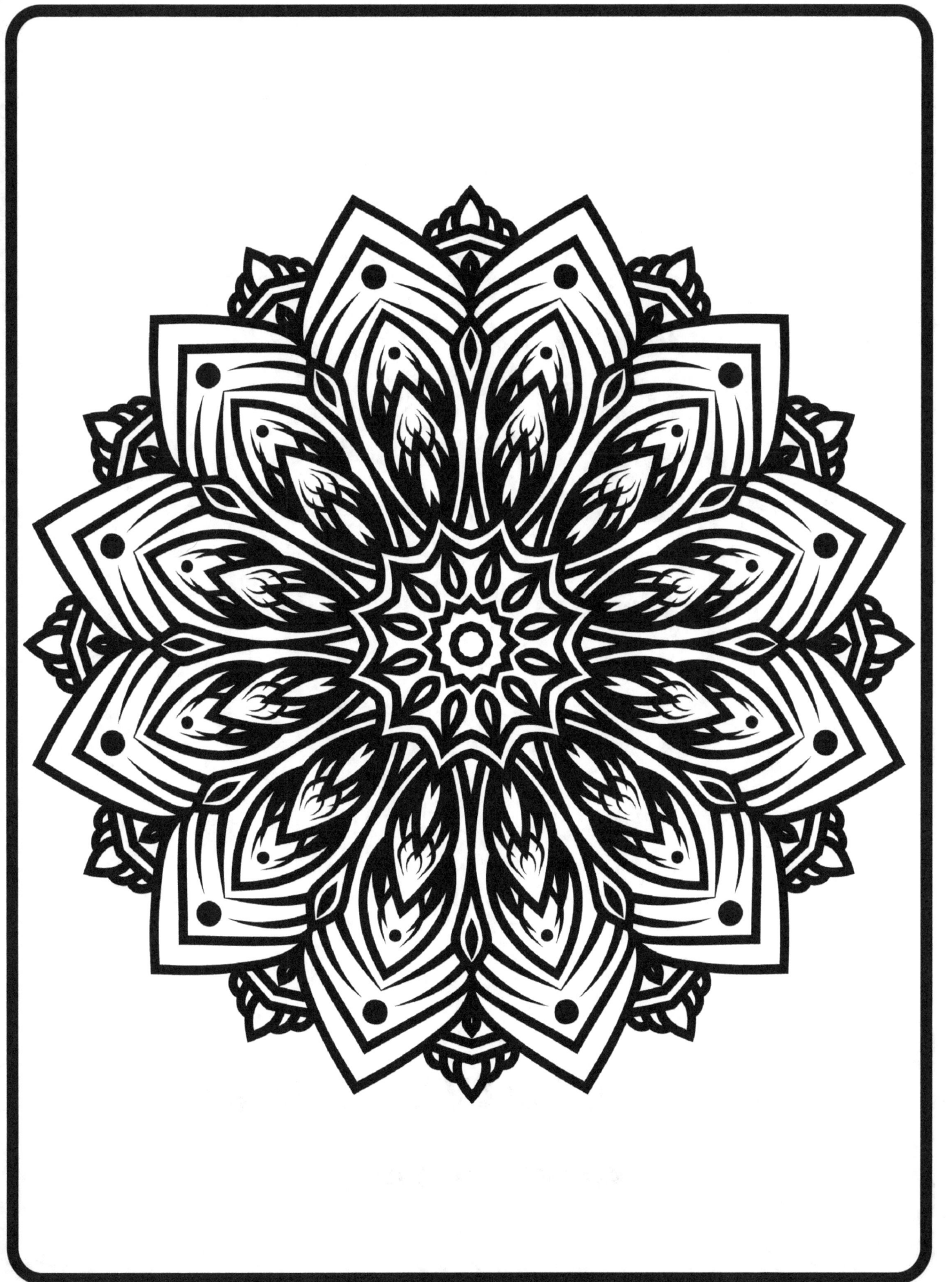

INTENTIONALLY LEFT BLANK

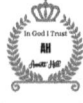 **ANNETT HILL**

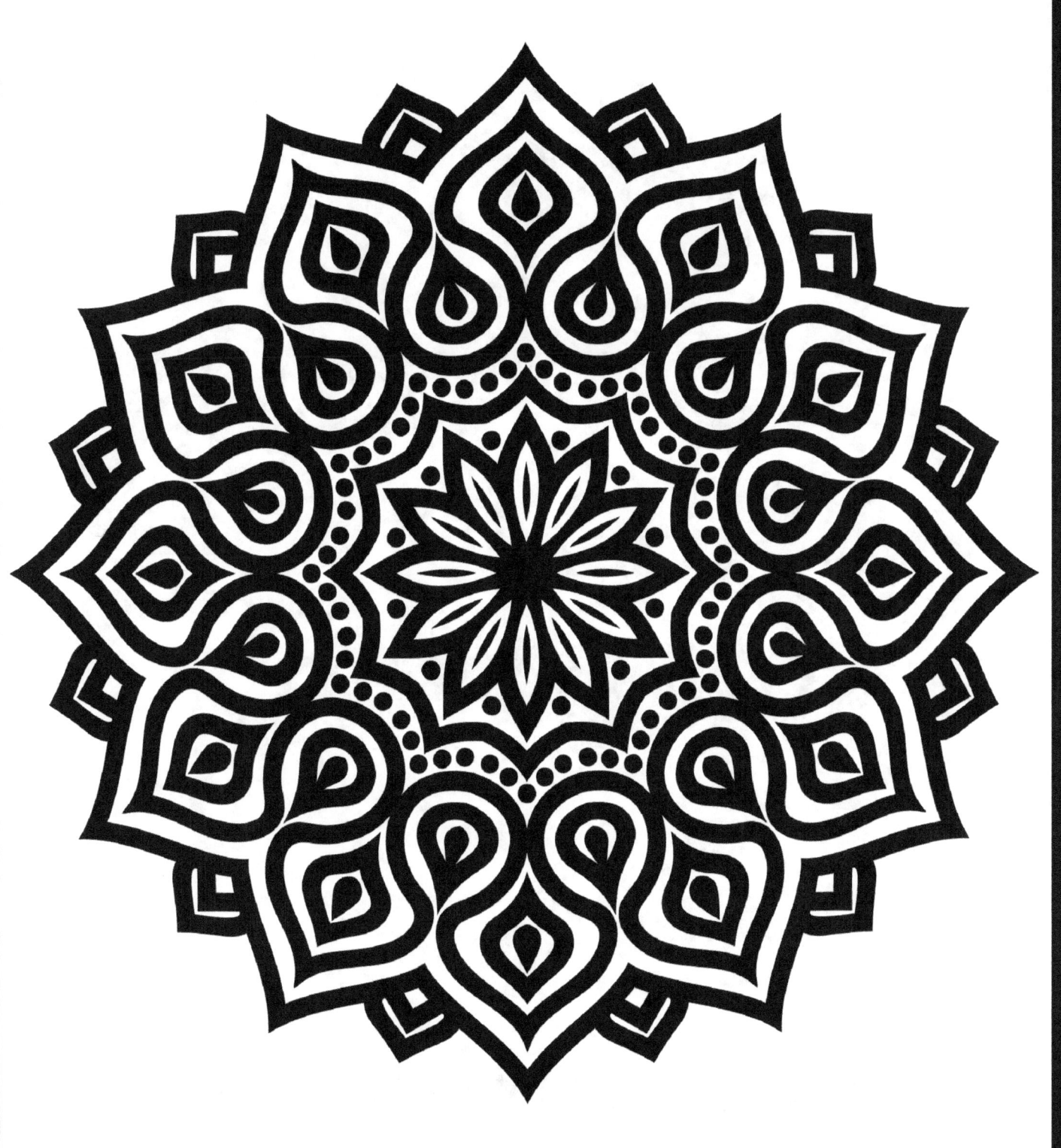

INTENTIONALLY LEFT BLANK

 ANNETT HILL

INTENTIONALLY LEFT BLANK

 **ANNETT HILL**

INTENTIONALLY LEFT BLANK

 ANNETT HILL

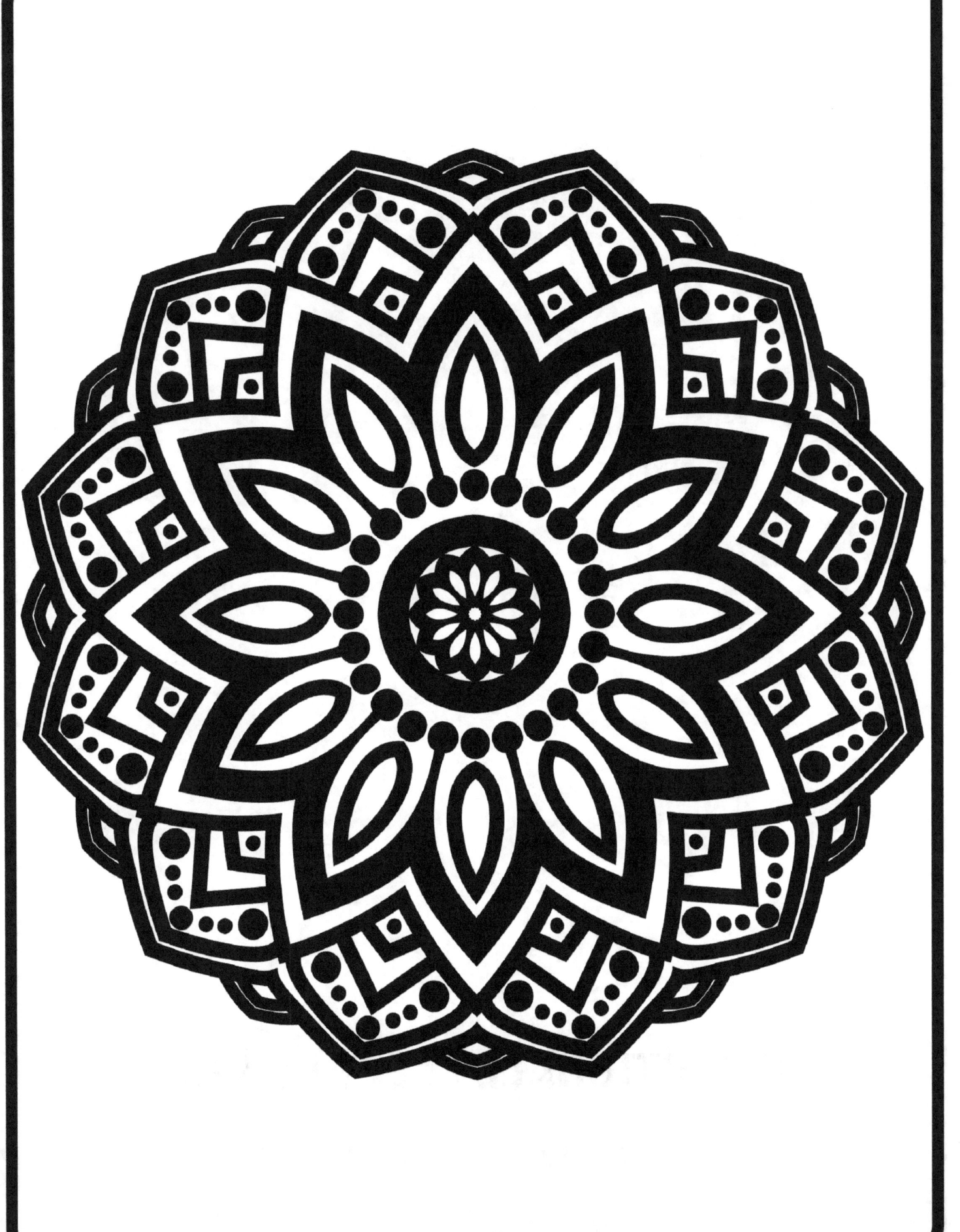

INTENTIONALLY LEFT BLANK

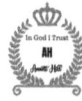 ANNETT HILL

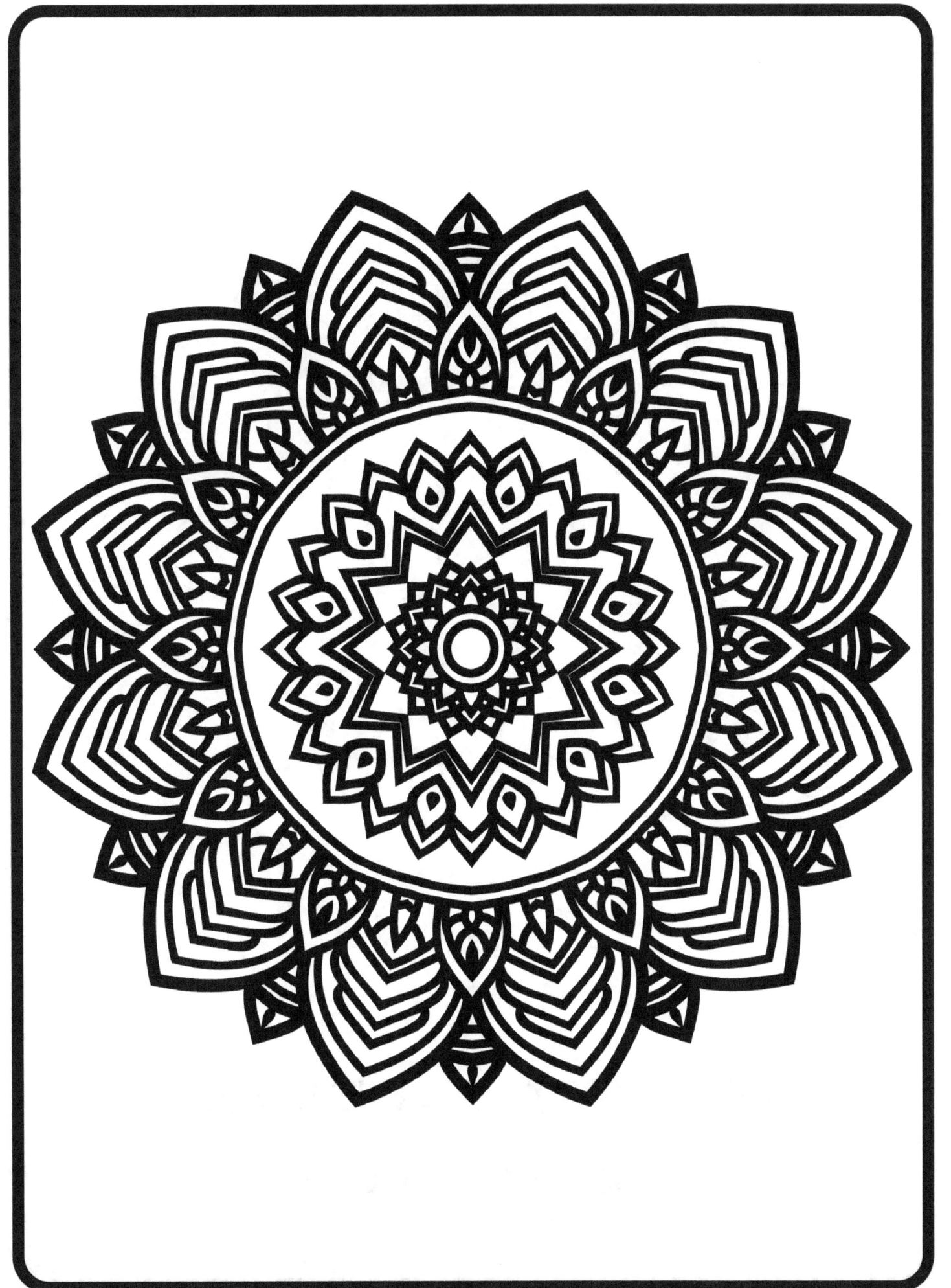

INTENTIONALLY LEFT BLANK

 ANNETT HILL

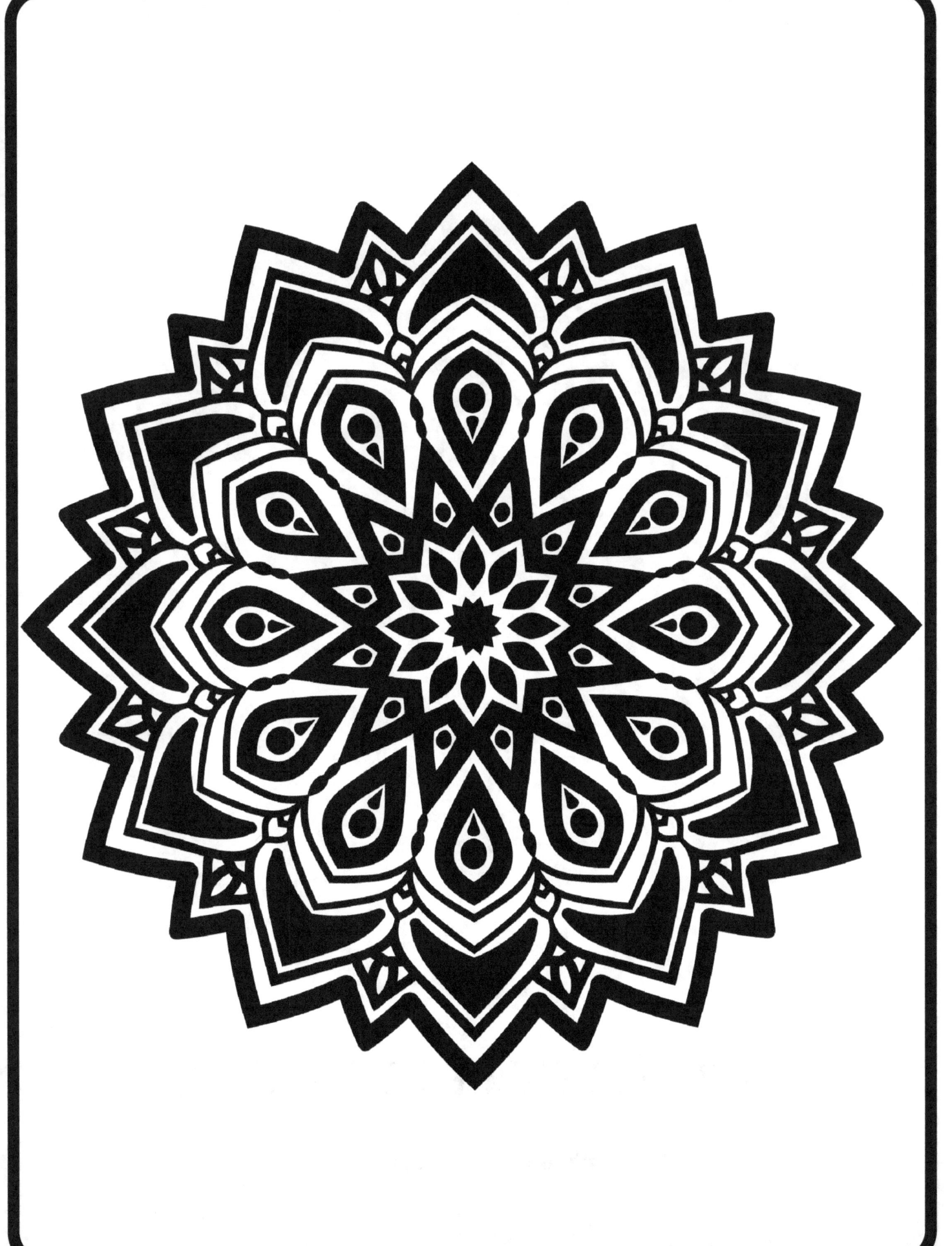

INTENTIONALLY LEFT BLANK

 ANNETT HILL

INTENTIONALLY LEFT BLANK

 ANNETT HILL

INTENTIONALLY LEFT BLANK

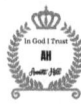 **ANNETT HILL**

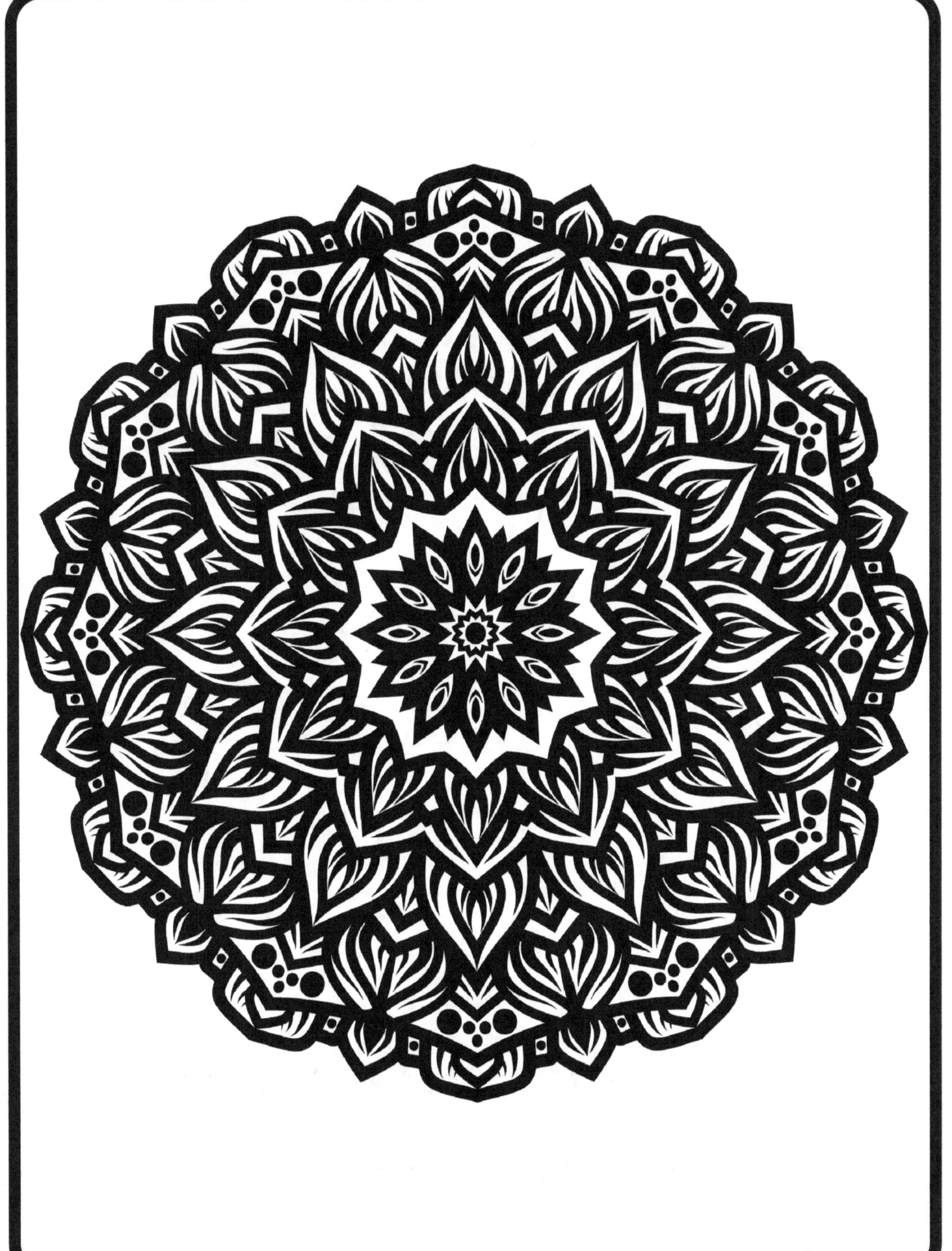

INTENTIONALLY LEFT BLANK

 ANNETT HILL

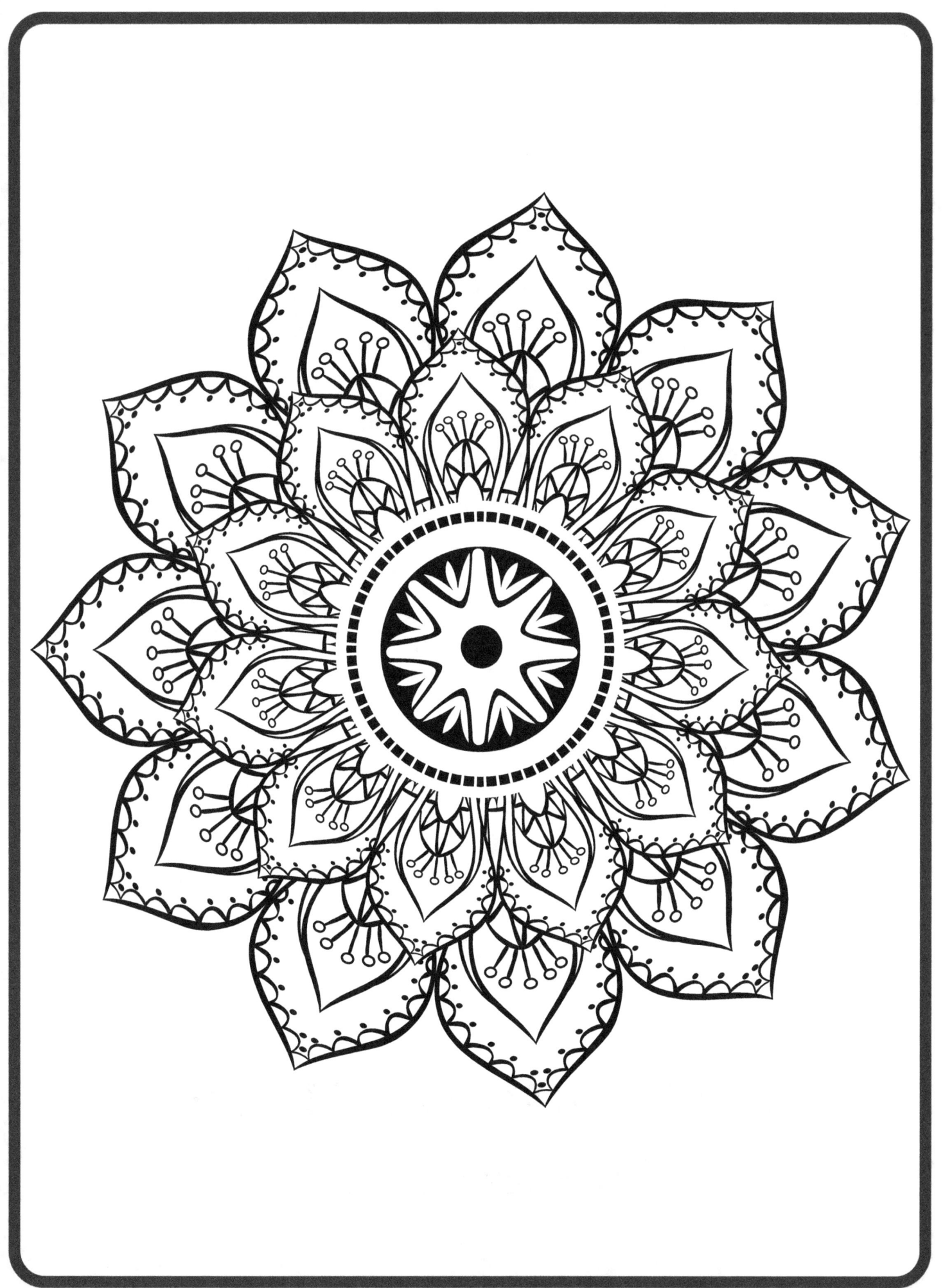

INTENTIONALLY LEFT BLANK

 **ANNETT HILL**

INTENTIONALLY LEFT BLANK

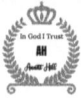 ANNETT HILL

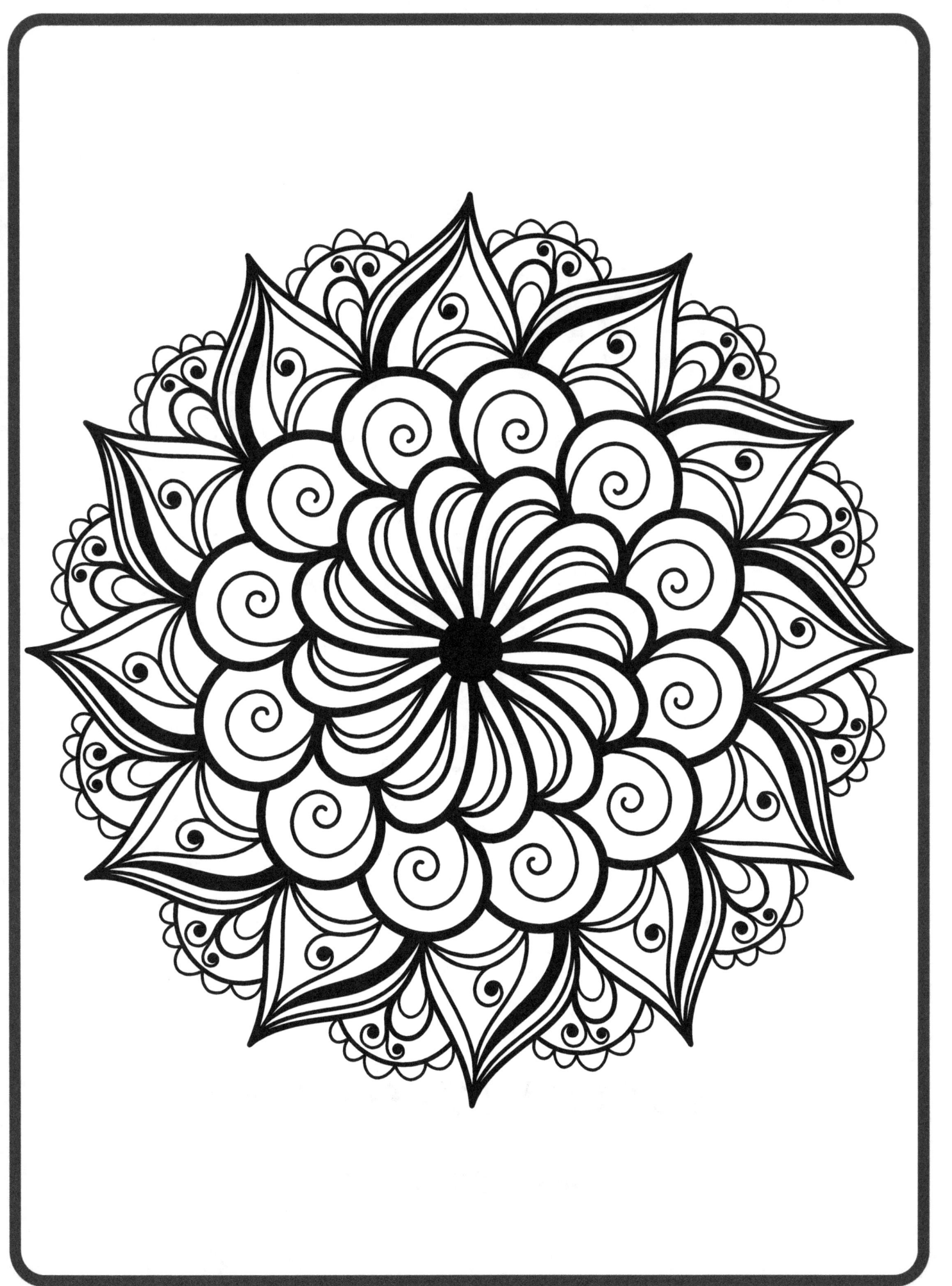

INTENTIONALLY LEFT BLANK

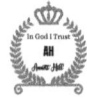 ANNETT HILL

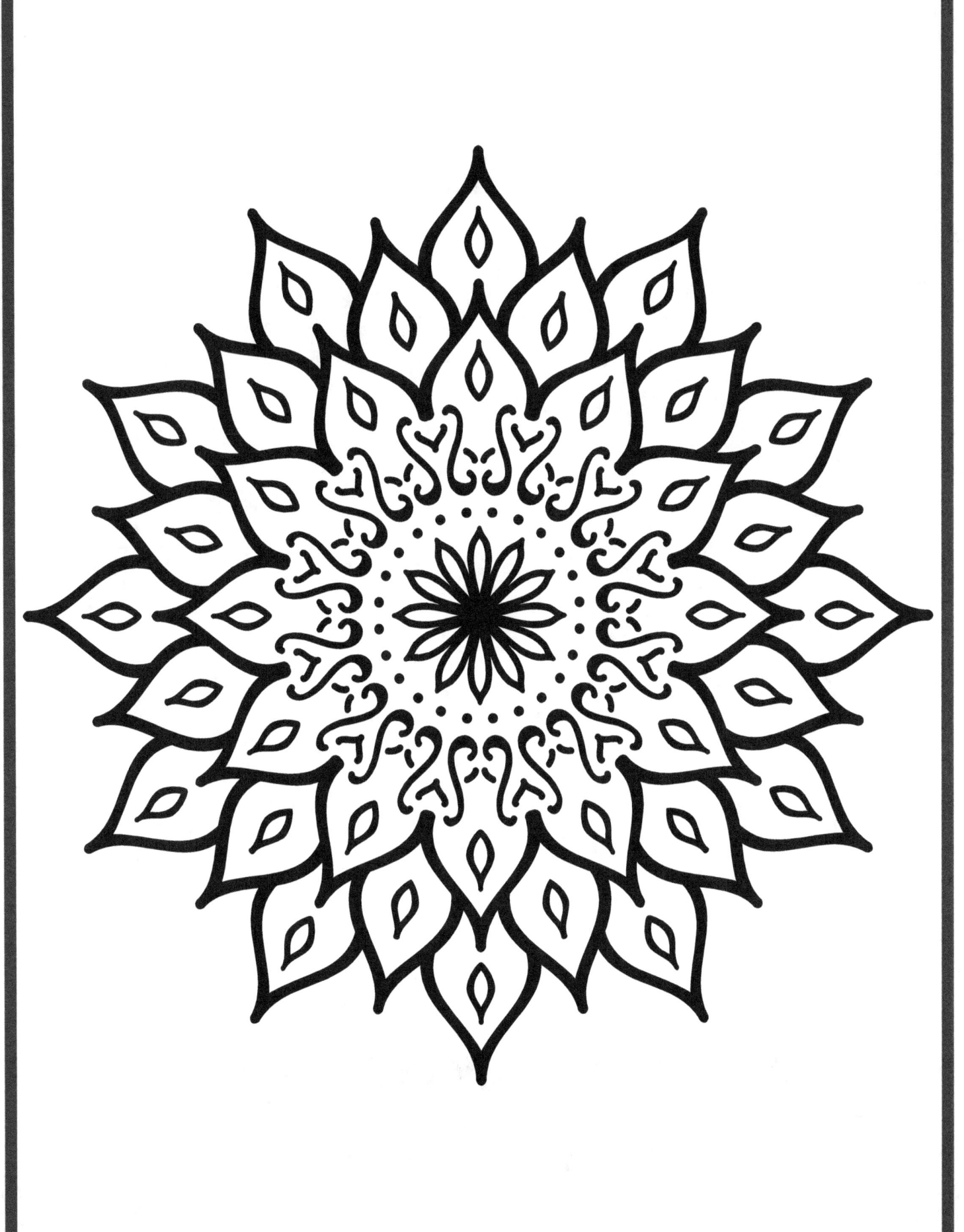

INTENTIONALLY LEFT BLANK

 ANNETT HILL

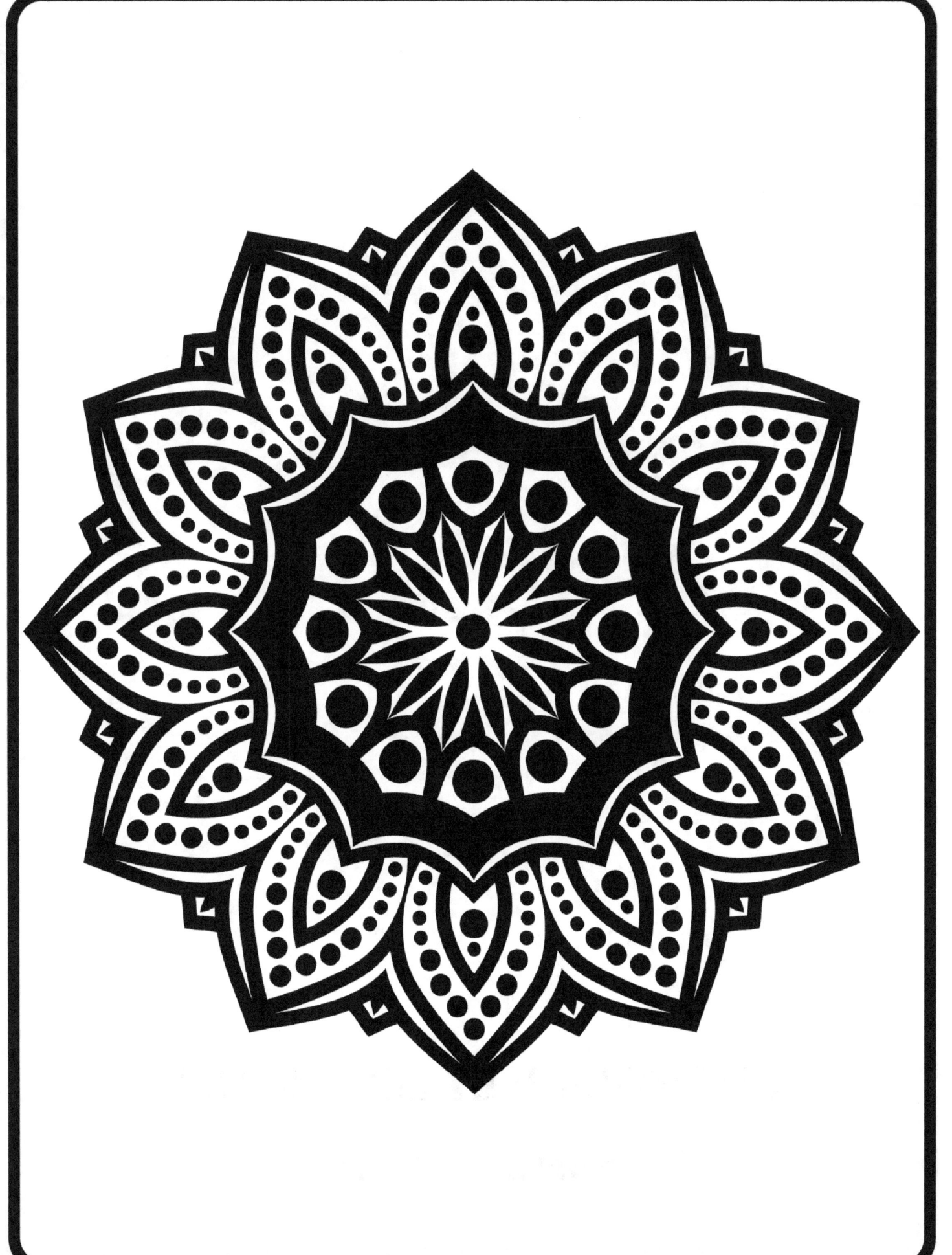

INTENTIONALLY LEFT BLANK

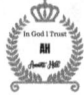 **ANNETT HILL**

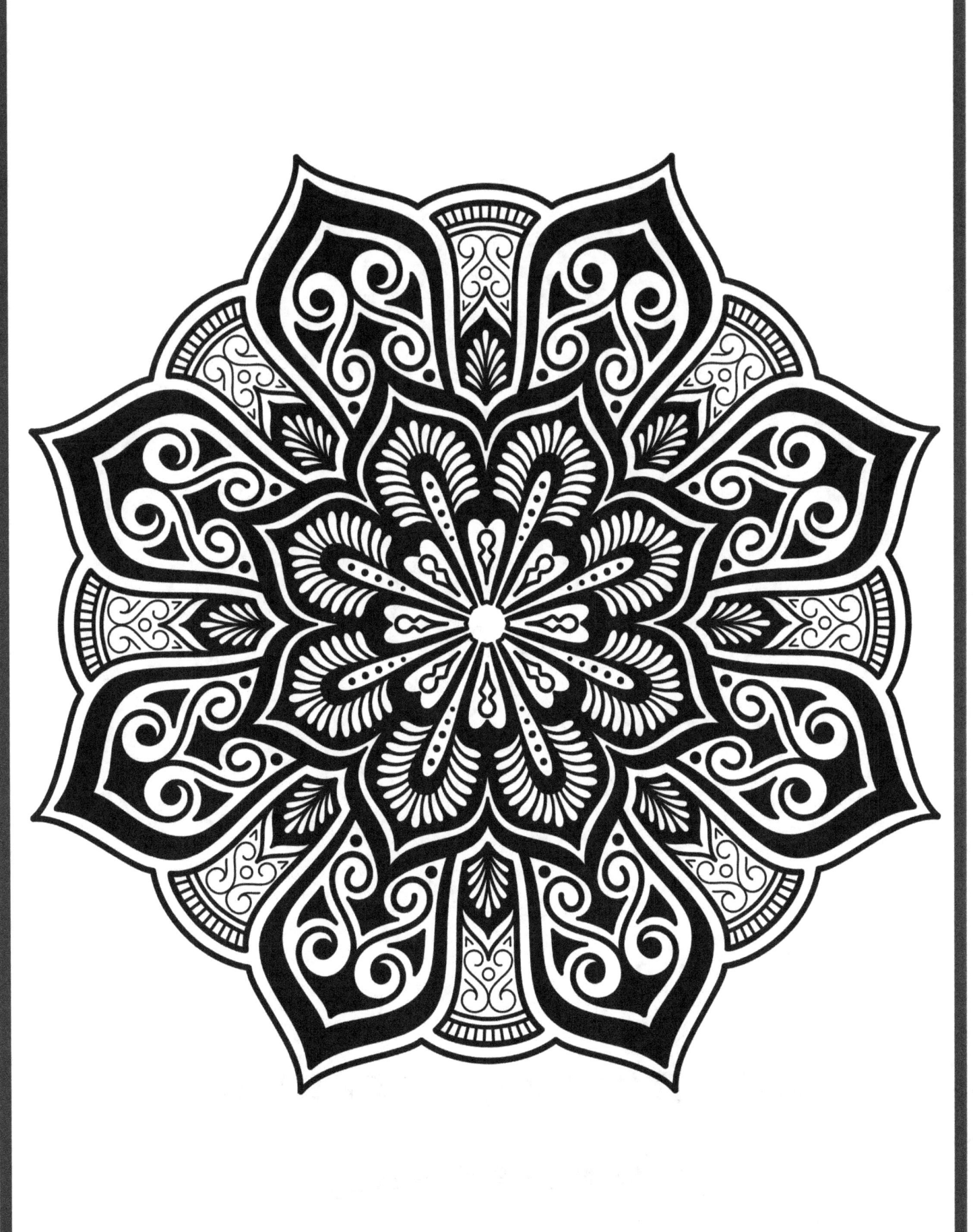

INTENTIONALLY LEFT BLANK

 ANNETT HILL

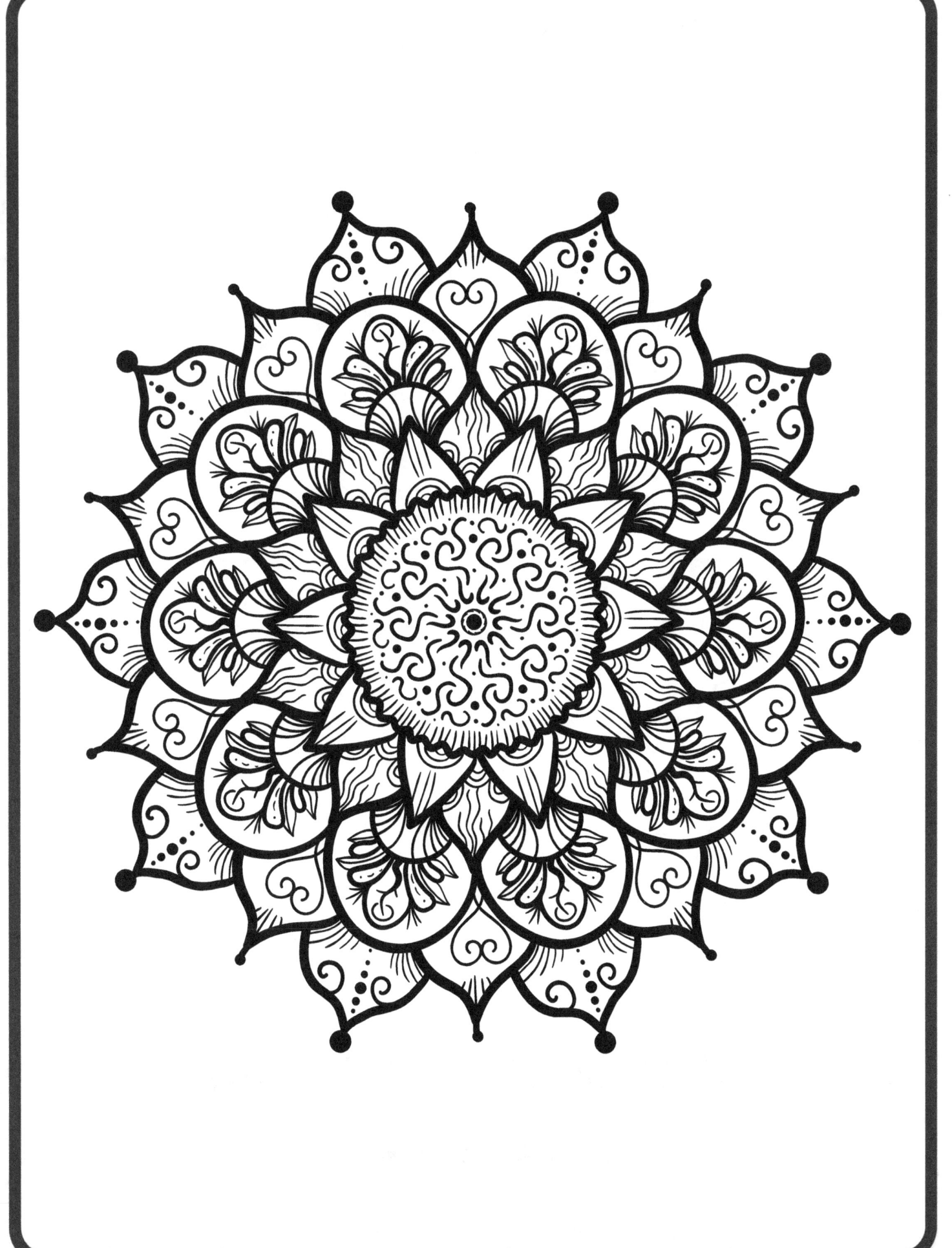

INTENTIONALLY LEFT BLANK

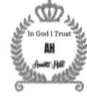 **ANNETT HILL**

www.ingramcontent.com/pod-product-compliance
Lightning Source LLC
Chambersburg PA
CBHW080845220526
45467CB00008B/2393